THE WORLD'S BEST FOOTBALL STORIES

Fun & Inspirational Facts & Stories of the Greatest Football Players and Games of All Time

FALCON FOCUS

Copyright © 2023 Falcon Focus

All rights reserved. No part of this publication may be reproduced, distributed or transmitted in any form or by any means, including photocopying, recording, or other electronic or mechanical methods, without the prior written permission of the publisher, except in the case of brief quotations embodied in critical reviews and certain other non-commercial uses permitted by copyright law.

Trademarked names appear throughout this book. Rather than use a trademark symbol with every occurrence of a trademarked name, names are used in an editorial fashion, with no intention of infringement of the respective owner's trademark. The information in this book is distributed on an "as is" basis, without warranty. Although every precaution has been taken in the preparation of this work, neither the author nor the publisher shall have any liability to any person or entity with respect to any loss or damage caused or alleged to be caused directly or indirectly by the information contained in this book.

American football is more than a game; it's a saga played out on a field of green. Every snap is a story, every tackle a triumph, and every pass a piece of art painted in the air. In this arena, every touchdown is a tale of teamwork, every field goal a feat of precision, and every play a dance of strategy and strength. On this gridiron, legends are born, resilience is tested, and every yard gained is a step toward glory etched in the memories of both players and spectators.

Contents

Introduction	v
1. Devin Hester's Record Returns	1
2. Tom Brady: The Sixth Round Pick	9
3. The Reggie White Effect	18
4. The Greatest Show on Turf	25
5. Jason Witten: The Iron Man	33
6. Vince Lombardi's Leadership	40
7. Doug Williams: Breaking Barriers	48
8. The 12th Man	54
9. The Miracle at the Super Bowl	61
10. Walter Payton's Grace	68
11. Peyton Manning's Comeback	75
12. The Immaculate Reception	82
13. Sarah Fuller's Historic Kick	89
14. The Ice Bowl	96
15. Derrick Coleman's Inspiring Journey	103
16. The Legend of Jerry Rice	110
17. The Iron Will of Brett Favre	117
18. The Revolutionary Tony Dungy	124
References	131
Bonus: Free Book!	133

Introduction

Welcome, football enthusiasts, to a world brimming with the thrills, challenges, and unforgettable moments of football! *The World's Best Football Stories* is a journey into the heart of the game, exploring the dedication, resilience, and spirit that define some of football's most remarkable figures.

As you delve into these pages, you will encounter the incredible story of Tom Brady, the sixth-round draft pick who became an NFL legend, and feel the electrifying excitement of Devin Hester's record-setting returns. You'll be inspired by the enduring impact of Reggie White, both as a dominant player and a man of character, and relive the dynamic plays of "The Greatest Show on Turf."

Witness the resilience and reliability of Jason Witten, known as the Iron Man of football, and revisit the miraculous comeback led by Tom Brady in the Super Bowl. Learn from the leadership lessons of Vince Lombardi, a coach who shaped the game with his wisdom and vision. Experience the groundbreaking journey of Doug Williams, who shattered barriers and redefined what it means to be a quarterback.

Each story in this collection goes beyond the field, revealing the human side of football – the triumphs, the struggles, and the unwavering spirit of those who love the game. Whether you're a young player, a dedicated fan, or someone who appreciates a compelling story, these tales are for you. So, gear up, get ready to cheer, and embark on a journey that captures the essence of football and the lessons it teaches us about life. Let's explore together the magic and inspiration that football brings to people around the world!

Devin Hester's Record Returns

Early Life and Career Beginnings

Devin Hester's journey to becoming one of the most electrifying return specialists in NFL history began far from the bright lights of professional stadiums. Born on November 4, 1982, in Riviera Beach, Florida, Hester's early life was shaped by his surroundings and experiences in a neighborhood where positive outlets were essential for young people.

From a young age, Hester exhibited a natural athleticism and a passion for sports. He grew up playing a variety of sports, but it was football where his speed and agility truly shone. These early years were not just about physical development; they were also about nurturing a love for the game that would become his career.

Hester attended Suncoast High School in Riviera Beach, where he quickly made a name for himself as a standout athlete. He excelled not only in football but also in track and field, showcasing the speed that would later become his trademark in the NFL. His high school football career was marked by spectacular plays that saw him playing multiple positions, including wide receiver, defensive back, and return specialist.

His performance in high school caught the attention of several college scouts, and Hester eventually chose to attend the University of Miami, a school known for its prestigious football program. At Miami, Hester continued to showcase his extraordinary talents. He became known for his explosive speed, agility, and an uncanny ability to read the field, making him a threat every time he touched the ball.

Hester's college career was highlighted by numerous memorable plays that gave glimpses of what he would eventually bring to the NFL. He played various roles on the team, further demonstrating his versatility and raw athletic ability. However, it was as a return specialist that Hester truly began to stand out. His ability to turn seemingly routine kick and punt returns into game-changing plays made him a standout player at Miami.

Specialization in Returns

The role of a return specialist is unique and highly specialized. It requires more than just raw speed. A return specialist must have excellent vision to identify and exploit gaps in the opposing team's coverage. They must possess exceptional decision-making skills to determine when to field the ball, when to let it go, and how to navigate through the narrowest of openings. Hester honed these abilities, combining his physical gifts with a deep understanding of return strategies.

Hester's ability to anticipate the movements of opposing players set him apart. This skill was not just innate; it was sharpened through countless hours of studying film and understanding opponents' tendencies. His instincts allowed him to make split-second decisions during returns, often leading to spectacular results.

Being a return specialist also involves risk management. Hester had to assess the risks of fielding punts in different situations, balancing the potential for a game-changing return with the safety of securing possession. His judgment in these moments was exemplary, often making the right call between taking a chance for a big return and opting for the safer play.

Hester's presence on the field transformed the special teams unit of any team he played for. Opponents had to plan specifically for him, often altering their usual kicking strategies to avoid giving him return opportunities. This strategic impact demonstrated the value Hester brought beyond his individual performances.

In the NFL, Hester quickly established himself as a formidable return specialist. He set numerous records, including the most punt return touchdowns and the most total return touchdowns, a testament to his effectiveness and impact in this role.

To excel as a return specialist, Hester maintained rigorous training and conditioning. He worked on enhancing his speed and agility, crucial attributes for maneuvering through the tight spaces and rapid changes of direction required in returns. His physical preparation was tailored to maintain his explosive athleticism, a key factor in his success.

Lastly, the role of a return specialist required mental toughness. It's a high-pressure role where a single mistake can be costly. Hester's ability to maintain focus, withstand pressure, and bounce back from any setbacks was central to his success.

Key Games and Returns

Devin Hester's career is studded with numerous breathtaking returns, each showcasing his extraordinary ability as a return specialist. Some of these key games and returns not only highlight his individual talent but also had significant impacts on the games and, in some cases, on the Chicago Bears' and Atlanta Falcons' seasons.

NFL Debut - September 10, 2006: Hester announced his arrival in the NFL in dramatic fashion. In his first regular-season game against the Green Bay Packers, he returned a punt 84 yards for a touchdown. This debut return was a sign of things to come and instantly put the league on notice.

Super Bowl XLI - February 4, 2007: Perhaps the most iconic moment of Hester's career came in Super Bowl XLI against the Indianapolis Colts. He opened the game with a stunning 92-yard kickoff return for a touchdown, the first and only time a Super Bowl has started with a kickoff return for a touchdown. This play not only electrified the Bears but also etched Hester's name in Super Bowl history.

- October 16, 2011: Hester set the NFL record for the most punt return touchdowns in a career in this game against the Minnesota Vikings. He returned a punt 98 yards for a touchdown, showcasing his incredible speed and agility. This return was a historic moment, solidifying Hester's status as one of the greatest return specialists of all time.
- November 25, 2007: In a game against the Denver Broncos, Hester showcased his versatility and threat on special teams with two remarkable returns for touchdowns – one a 75-yard punt return and another a 69-yard kickoff return. These back-to-back returns were pivotal in the Bears' victory and highlighted Hester's game-changing abilities.
- September 18, 2011: Against the New Orleans Saints, Hester returned a punt 81 yards for a touchdown, displaying his signature combination of speed, vision, and agility. This return was a classic example of Hester's ability to break open a game with a single play.
- October 2, 2006: In a Monday Night Football game against the Arizona Cardinals, Hester's 88-yard punt return for a touchdown was a critical play in one of the most memorable comebacks in NFL history. The Bears overcame a 20-point deficit, in part due to Hester's electrifying return.
- November 13, 2011: Against the Detroit Lions, Hester's 62-yard punt return for a touchdown demonstrated his consistent threat in the return game. His ability to find gaps in the coverage and exploit them was on full display in this return.

Each of these key returns by Devin Hester not only contributed significantly to his team's performance but also left an indelible mark on the NFL. His returns were not just about scoring; they were momentum-shifters that could change the complexion of a game. Hester's ability to consistently produce such game-changing plays made him a unique and unforgettable player in the league.

Challenges and Overcoming Them

Devin Hester's illustrious career as a return specialist was not without its challenges. Despite his extraordinary abilities, Hester faced several obstacles throughout his career, which he had to overcome to maintain his status as one of the greatest in his position.

One of the initial challenges Hester faced was the transition from college football to the NFL. The speed, complexity, and overall level of play in the NFL were a significant step up from college. Hester had to quickly adapt to this higher level of competition and learn to apply his skills effectively against more sophisticated and challenging opponents.

Early in his career, the Chicago Bears attempted to utilize Hester's athleticism more broadly by converting him into a wide receiver. This shift presented a challenge as it required him to develop a new skill set, learn complex routes, and understand the nuances of a different position while still maintaining his prowess as a return specialist. The transition had mixed results and was a source of debate among analysts and fans regarding the best use of his talents.

The very role that brought Hester's fame also came with its challenges. As a return specialist, he was often the focus of special teams' defenses. Teams would kick away from him or employ various strategies to limit his impact, forcing Hester to continually adapt and find new ways to be effective.

Like many NFL players, Hester dealt with injuries throughout his career. The physical toll of being a return specialist, with high-speed collisions and tackles, posed a constant risk. Managing these injuries and maintaining his top physical condition was a continual challenge.

Hester's early success set a high bar. Maintaining this level of performance and living up to the expectations was a challenge, especially as opponents became more adept at countering his return abilities. The pressure to consistently perform at an elite level can be a significant burden for any athlete.

As Hester's career progressed, his role on teams began to change. Teams increasingly saw him more as a veteran presence and less as the primary return threat. Adapting to these changing roles, especially towards the end of his career with the Atlanta Falcons and Baltimore Ravens, was a challenge as it required him to find new ways to contribute to his team's success.

Impact on the Game

Hester's impact on the game of football, particularly on special teams play, was profound and far-reaching. His exceptional skills as a return specialist not only brought excitement to kick and punt returns but also fundamentally changed how teams approached these aspects of the game.

Hester's presence on the field had a significant psychological impact on opposing teams. Knowing his capability to turn any return into a touchdown, many teams altered their kicking strategies to avoid giving him opportunities. This often meant deliberately kicking out of bounds or using high, short kicks to reduce the chances of a return, which could result in less favorable field positions for them. Hester's impact was such that he effectively changed the tactical approach teams used in special teams' play.

Hester's success brought a renewed focus and importance to the special teams' unit. He demonstrated that a dynamic return specialist could be a game-changer, leading teams to invest more in scouting and developing talent in this area. The emphasis on special teams performance increased across the league, with teams looking for their own version of a return threat like Hester.

Devin became a role model for aspiring return specialists. His style, success, and the excitement he brought to the field inspired many young players to specialize in returns. He showed that this role could be more than just a team utility but a position of significant impact and star power.

Hester's ability to consistently provide his team with excellent field position highlighted the strategic importance of kick and punt returns in football. He brought attention to how effective special teams play could influence the momentum of the game and contribute to a team's overall success.

Coaches were compelled to innovate and develop new strategies to contain returners like Hester. This led to advancements in how special teams were coached, with more emphasis on coverage schemes, tackling techniques, and kick placement. Hester's influence pushed teams to be more strategic and precise in their special teams coaching.

Hester set new standards for what teams expect from their return specialists. His record-breaking performances established benchmarks for measuring success in return yards and touchdowns, becoming goals for other players in similar roles.

Lessons for Young Athletes

Devin Hester's remarkable career as a return specialist offers valuable lessons for young athletes, particularly about the importance of finding and excelling in a specific niche. His journey and success demonstrate several key principles that aspiring athletes can learn from.

Hester's career is a prime example of recognizing and capitalizing on one's natural talents. He identified his exceptional speed and agility as his key strengths and honed them to perfection. Young athletes can learn the importance of self-awareness in their athletic journey, understanding what they are good at and focusing on these areas to excel.

In a world where versatility in sports is often praised, Hester showed that specializing in a specific area could lead to extraordinary success. He dedicated himself to mastering the art of returns, which eventually made him one of the most feared players in the NFL. Young athletes can see the benefits of becoming exceptionally skilled in a particular aspect of their sport.

Hester's achievements weren't just due to his natural abilities; they were also a product of his incredible work ethic and dedication to improving. He spent countless hours practicing, studying, and perfecting his craft. This commitment serves as a lesson to young athletes that while talent is important, hard work and dedication are what truly unlock an athlete's potential.

Throughout his career, Hester faced challenges, including adapting to the NFL's level of play and dealing with strategic changes by opponents. His ability to adapt and overcome these challenges is a valuable lesson for young athletes in resilience and flexibility.

Hester's success as a return specialist was not just due to his physical skills but also his understanding of the game. His ability to read plays and anticipate opponents' actions was crucial. Young athletes can learn from this that excelling in sports is not just about physical abilities but also about mental acuity and understanding the strategic aspects of the game.

Hester's excellence in his niche role inspired others and changed how teams approached special teams. Young athletes can see the potential impact they can have by excelling in their roles, inspiring their teammates, and contributing to the overall success of their teams.

As his career progressed, Hester's role on teams evolved. He embraced these changes, finding new ways to contribute and stay relevant. This adaptability is a crucial lesson for young athletes in understanding that roles can change and being prepared to adapt is key to a long and successful athletic career.

Devin Hester's career offers rich lessons for young athletes. It underscores the importance of recognizing one's unique talents, dedicating oneself to mastering a specific aspect of the game, and the need for hard work, adaptability, and a deep understanding of the strategic elements of the sport. His journey is a testament to how specializing in a niche can lead to remarkable success and a lasting legacy in the world of sports.

Tom Brady: The Sixth Round Pick

Early Career and Draft

Tom Brady's journey to becoming one of the greatest quarterbacks in NFL history is a remarkable tale of perseverance and belief in oneself, beginning with an often overlooked and undervalued start. Born on August 3, 1977, in San Mateo, California, Brady nurtured his passion for football from a young age, idolizing players like Joe Montana and dreaming of one day playing in the NFL. His early years were marked by a deep dedication to the sport, playing as a quarterback for Junipero Serra High School in San Mateo.

Despite his early passion and commitment, Brady was not a standout star in high school. He was good, but not exceptional in the eyes of many college scouts. His journey to the University of Michigan as a quarterback was the first step in a career characterized by patience and resilience. At Michigan, Brady found himself seventh on the depth chart and struggled to get playing time. However, his determination never waned. He spent hours studying game films, working on his technique, and preparing mentally and physically for the opportunity to lead his team. By his junior year, he had fought his way up to be the starting quarterback.

Brady's college career was marked by significant improvement and moments of brilliance, yet doubts persisted among NFL scouts. His NFL Combine performance in 2000 did little to quell these doubts. He was not particularly fast, his arm strength was questioned, and his physical build was deemed less than ideal for an NFL quarterback. These factors contributed to Brady being largely overlooked in the 2000 NFL Draft.

As the draft progressed, Brady watched as quarterback after quarterback was chosen ahead of him. The experience was emotionally taxing. He later recounted the disappointment and frustration he felt as he waited for his name to be called, a wait that seemed endless and disheartening. In an interview, Brady shared how he stepped outside his family's house, fighting back tears, trying to come to terms with the uncertainty of his football future.

Finally, in the sixth round, with the 199th overall pick, the New England Patriots selected Tom Brady. This selection was not celebrated with great fanfare. Few could have predicted that this sixth-round pick would go on to redefine success in the NFL. For Brady, it was both a relief and a new beginning, a chance to prove his worth in a league that had largely undervalued his potential.

The draft experience instilled in Brady a chip on his shoulder, a relentless drive to prove not just to the world, but to himself, that he was more than just a sixth-round pick. It was this drive, born from the uncertainty and disappointment of his draft experience, that would fuel his legendary NFL career.

Consistency and Durability

Upon joining the New England Patriots, Brady quickly began to demonstrate his unwavering commitment to the game. He embraced a rigorous fitness and nutrition regimen, one that he would refine and adhere to throughout his career. This dedication to his physical well-being was a key factor in his remarkable longevity in the league. Brady's approach went beyond traditional training methods; he focused on pliability, nutrition, hydration, and mental training, which helped him stay at the top of his game well into his 40s, a rare feat in the physically demanding world of professional football.

Brady's record for consecutive starts is a testament to his durability. He began his starting role in the 2001 season, after an injury to then-starter Drew Bledsoe. From that moment, Brady seized the opportunity and never looked back. He led the Patriots to their first Super Bowl victory that season and established himself as an irreplaceable asset to the team. His ability to consistently perform at a high level, game after game, season after season, set him apart from his peers.

One of the most significant aspects of Brady's career has been his ability to avoid serious injury. Apart from the 2008 season, when he suffered a knee injury in the opening game and missed the remainder of the season, Brady has been remarkably injury-free. This is no small feat in the NFL, where the physical toll on players, especially quarterbacks, is immense. Brady's commitment to his off-season and in-season training played a crucial role in this. He worked tirelessly on strengthening his body, understanding that durability was just as important as skill in ensuring a long and successful career.

Furthermore, Brady's mental toughness and ability to perform under pressure contributed greatly to his consistency. He was known for his cool demeanor in high-stress situations, often leading his team to victory in the final minutes of the game. This mental fortitude, combined with his physical preparedness, made him one of the most reliable players in the league.

Over the years, Brady's consistency has been a cornerstone of the Patriots' dynasty. He led the team to nine Super Bowl appearances, winning six of them. His longevity and consistent high-level performance are unparalleled, earning him the respect of teammates, coaches, and opponents alike.

In an era where player movement is common, and careers can be cut short by injury, Brady's consistency and durability stand as a shining example. He redefined what it means to be a quarterback in the NFL, not just through his skill and leadership but through his extraordinary ability to remain at the peak of his game for over two decades.

Challenges and Resilience

Tom Brady's journey to becoming one of the greatest quarterbacks in NFL history was not without its fair share of challenges. From internal competition within his team to widespread public skepticism, Brady faced numerous obstacles that tested his resilience and determination.

When Brady joined the New England Patriots, he was not immediately seen as a star player. He started as the fourth-string quarterback and had to work tirelessly to prove himself. The competition within the team was intense. Brady was up against established players, including Drew Bledsoe, a highly regarded and well-established quarterback. The challenge for Brady was not just to match the physical skills of his competitors but to demonstrate a unique value that he could bring to the team.

Brady's opportunity came in the 2001 season when Bledsoe was injured. Brady stepped in and quickly proved his worth, leading the team to victory after victory. However, even with this success, there were doubts about whether he could sustain this level of performance. The initial view of many was that Brady was a temporary solution, a stop-gap until Bledsoe returned. Yet, Brady continued to excel, turning skepticism into admiration and eventually becoming the team's undisputed starting quarterback.

Another significant challenge Brady faced was public skepticism. Early in his career, he was often viewed as a system quarterback, one who succeeded due to the Patriots' system rather than his own abilities. This perception was fueled by the team's continued success, regardless of the individual players in the lineup. Brady had to constantly prove that his success was not just a product of the system but a result of his skill, intelligence, and hard work.

The "Deflategate" scandal was another challenge that tested Brady's resilience. He faced accusations of having knowingly used under-inflated footballs in the 2015 AFC Championship Game against the Indianapolis Colts. This controversy led to a four-game suspension at the start of the 2016 season. The incident was a significant challenge to Brady's reputation and legacy. However, he responded by maintaining his innocence, staying focused on the game, and returning to lead the Patriots to another Super Bowl victory in the same season.

Throughout his career, Brady also faced the challenge of evolving with the game and adapting to new team dynamics as players and coaches came and went. His ability to continually adjust his style of play to fit new strategies and teammates showcased not only his physical ability but also his mental acuity and adaptability.

Brady's resilience in the face of these challenges is a key part of his legacy. He did not allow competition, skepticism, or controversy to derail his focus or commitment to the sport. Instead, he used these challenges as fuel to further enhance his performance and cement his status as one of the greatest quarterbacks in NFL history.

Achievements

Tom Brady's list of achievements and accolades is extensive, marking him as one of the most accomplished players in NFL history. His career is studded with remarkable milestones, from Super Bowl victories to numerous NFL records.

Brady's most notable achievements are his seven Super Bowl victories, the most by any player in NFL history. These wins came in Super Bowls XXXVI, XXXVIII, XXXIX, XLIX, LI, LIII, and LV. Each victory highlighted different stages of Brady's career and showcased his ability to lead his team to success under varying circumstances.

- Super Bowl XXXVI (2002): Brady's first Super Bowl win came against the St. Louis Rams. Then a young quarterback, he led a game-winning drive in the final minutes, beginning his legacy as a clutch performer.
- Super Bowl XXXVIII (2004) and XXXIX (2005): These consecutive wins against the Carolina Panthers and Philadelphia Eagles solidified the Patriots' status as a dynasty and Brady's reputation as an elite quarterback.
- Super Bowl XLIX (2015): Against the Seattle Seahawks, Brady orchestrated another late-game comeback, further cementing his legacy.

- Super Bowl LI (2017): Perhaps his most remarkable Super Bowl performance, Brady led the Patriots to overcome a 28-3 deficit against the Atlanta Falcons, the largest comeback in Super Bowl history.
- Super Bowl LIII (2019): A win against the Los Angeles Rams, this victory was a testament to Brady's longevity and sustained excellence.
- Super Bowl LV (2021): Winning with the Tampa Bay Buccaneers, Brady proved his ability to achieve the pinnacle of success outside of the New England Patriots' system.

In addition to his Super Bowl victories, Brady has numerous NFL records. Some of his most significant records include:

- Brady holds the record for the most career wins by an NFL quarterback.
- He has thrown more touchdown passes than any other quarterback in NFL history.
- Brady has amassed the most passing yards in NFL history.

Brady has also been recognized with numerous individual awards. He is a three-time NFL Most Valuable Player (MVP), awarded in 2007, 2010, and 2017. He has been selected to 14 Pro Bowls, showcasing his consistent high-level performance over two decades.

Moreover, Brady's achievements extend beyond these statistics and accolades. He has set numerous playoff records, including most games played, most games won, and most touchdown passes. His postseason success is a significant part of his legacy, demonstrating his ability to perform at his best when the stakes are highest.

Work Ethic and Leadership

Tom Brady's exceptional work ethic and leadership have been central to his sustained success and the success of his teams. These qualities have not only defined his personal career but have also significantly impacted the culture and performance of every team he has been part of.

Brady's approach to preparation and training is legendary. He is known for being the first to arrive and the last to leave during training sessions, setting a standard for commitment and dedication. His meticulous attention to detail in studying game film, understanding opponents' strategies, and mastering the Patriots' and later the Buccaneers' playbooks, became a hallmark of his career. This relentless pursuit of excellence extended to his physical training and nutrition. Brady adopted a holistic approach to his health, integrating strict dietary plans and innovative training methods that focused on flexibility and longevity, rather than just strength and endurance. This approach not only prolonged his career but also served as a model for younger players.

Brady's mental preparation is as rigorous as his physical training. He spent countless hours studying the game, understanding the nuances, and preparing for every possible scenario. This level of preparation ensured that he was seldom caught off-guard on the field and could make rapid, intelligent decisions under pressure.

Beyond his personal preparation, Brady's leadership style significantly influenced his teams. He led by example, demonstrating what dedication and focus looked like. His ability to remain calm under pressure, maintain a positive attitude, and rally his team in tough situations was inspirational. Brady was not just a leader in terms of gameplay; he was a mentor to younger players, sharing his knowledge and experience and fostering a supportive team environment.

Brady's influence extended to the entire team culture. His high standards and commitment to excellence raised the bar for everyone around him. Teammates often spoke of how Brady's presence motivated them to work harder and perform better. This influence was particularly evident during critical moments in games, where Brady's composure and confidence had a calming effect on his teammates, enabling them to focus and perform at their best.

Brady's ability to adapt his leadership style to different teammates and situations was another key aspect of his success. Whether it was connecting with veteran players or guiding rookies, he knew how to communicate effectively and build strong relationships. This adaptability was crucial when he moved from the New England Patriots to the Tampa Bay

Buccaneers, where he successfully integrated into a new team and led them to a Super Bowl victory.

Tom Brady's work ethic and leadership were not just about setting personal records; they were about elevating the performance and mindset of his entire team. He instilled a culture of excellence, commitment, and resilience, which became the cornerstone of his teams' successes.

Legacy

Brady's influence on the sport of American football extends far beyond his impressive array of records and accolades. His legacy is one that has reshaped the narrative of what it means to be a successful athlete in the NFL and has provided invaluable lessons for young players aspiring to greatness.

Brady's career has redefined the quarterback role, showing that success at the position requires more than just physical skills. He demonstrated that mental acuity, game management, adaptability, and leadership are equally important. His ability to read defenses, adjust plays at the line of scrimmage, and maintain composure under pressure set new standards for quarterback performance.

Brady's success and longevity have had a profound impact on how teams view the quarterback position and the draft process. He challenged the notion that only high draft picks can become elite quarterbacks, showing that determination, work ethic, and continuous improvement are critical to success. His career has inspired teams to look beyond traditional metrics and consider the intangible qualities that contribute to a player's success.

Brady became a cultural icon, transcending the sport. His commitment to excellence and his personal story of overcoming odds have inspired countless fans and players. He has shown that with perseverance and dedication, it is possible to achieve one's dreams, regardless of where one starts.

Brady's career offers several lessons for young players. Firstly, it emphasizes the importance of a strong work ethic. Brady's dedication to training, preparation, and continual improvement is a blueprint for success. Secondly, it highlights the value of mental toughness and resilience. His ability to bounce back from setbacks, whether it be a poor draft position or on-field challenges, is a testament to his mental strength. Thirdly, Brady's career underscores the significance of adaptability and lifelong learning. He consistently adapted his play style and strategies to suit his team's needs and to stay competitive in a changing league.

Brady's approach to health and fitness, focusing on longevity and injury prevention, has influenced how athletes take care of their bodies. His advocacy for holistic wellness, including diet, mental health, and alternative training methods, has inspired players to consider how off-field habits impact their on-field performance.

Beyond his physical abilities, Brady has been a role model for leadership. His ability to inspire and lead his teammates, to set a high standard for performance, and to maintain a team-first attitude has set an example for what it means to be a leader in a team sport.

Tom Brady's legacy in the NFL is characterized by his transformation from an overlooked draft pick to one of the greatest players in the history of the sport. His career serves as an inspiring example of how dedication, resilience, and a commitment to continuous improvement can lead to extraordinary achievements. For young players, Brady's journey is a lesson in never underestimating the power of hard work, mental fortitude, and the relentless pursuit of one's goals.

The Reggie White Effect

Biography and Career Start

Reggie White, known as "The Minister of Defense," left an indelible mark on professional football. His prowess on the field and his impact off it are legendary. His journey from humble beginnings to becoming one of the most dominant defensive players in NFL history is a tale of talent, determination, and character.

Reggie White was born on December 19, 1961, in Chattanooga, Tennessee. From a young age, he displayed a deep passion for football. His physicality and athleticism made him stand out even as a youth. His early life was not just about sports. He was deeply involved in his faith, which played a significant role throughout his life and career.

In high school, White attended Howard High School in Chattanooga, where he first made a name for himself as a formidable defensive lineman. His performances there drew the attention of college scouts across the country. White chose to attend the University of Tennessee, where he continued to excel. At Tennessee, he set school records for sacks in a season and career sacks, a testament to his exceptional skill as a pass rusher and defensive player.

White's professional career began in the United States Football League (USFL) with the Memphis Showboats. There, he quickly established himself as a defensive force, showing the same intensity and effectiveness that he had displayed in college. When the USFL folded, White made the transition to the NFL, joining the Philadelphia Eagles in 1985.

White's arrival in the NFL was spectacular. He became an instant sensation with the Eagles, known for his extraordinary strength, speed, and technique. He wasn't just a pass rusher. He was a complete defensive lineman who could dominate against the run and the pass. His first few seasons with the Eagles saw him setting and breaking records, quickly becoming one of the most feared defenders in the league.

One of the hallmarks of White's early professional career was his versatility. He could play both inside and outside on the defensive line, a rarity and a tactical advantage for his team. His work ethic was legendary. He trained tirelessly to improve his strength, speed, and technique. White's dedication to his craft set a high standard for his teammates and made him a leader both on and off the field.

Dominance on the Field

Reggie White's time on the field was a masterclass in defensive play, marked by moments that have since become part of NFL folklore. His ability to take over games and impose his will against even the most formidable opponents was a spectacle that enthralled fans and earned the respect of fellow players.

One of the most remarkable aspects of White's play was his technique. He was known for his "hump move," a powerful maneuver where he would use his strength and quickness to throw blockers aside as if they were much lighter than their substantial weight. This move became one of White's signatures on the field, a testament to his unique combination of strength, speed, and technical prowess.

White's impact was also felt in the way he lifted the performance of his entire defensive unit. He was a leader who led by example, pushing his teammates to match his level of effort and commitment. The respect he commanded on the field was evident in the way other players looked to him for guidance and inspiration.

Off the field, White's influence was just as profound. His deep faith and commitment to community service made him a role model. He was actively involved in charitable work and often spoke about the importance of giving back to the community. This aspect of his life was as integral to his legacy as his achievements on the field.

The culmination of Reggie White's career achievements can be seen not just in the records he set or the games he dominated, but also in the way he changed the game of football. He set a new standard for defensive players, a benchmark that future generations would aspire to reach.

Leadership and team impact

Reggie White's influence as a leader on his teams was profound and multifaceted. He was not just a dominant force on the field but also a guiding light in the locker room and beyond, significantly shaping the culture and ethos of every team he was part of.

In terms of mentorship and guidance, White stood out as a figure of authority and wisdom. Young players often looked up to him, not only for advice on their game but also for guidance in their professional and personal lives. His willingness to share his knowledge and experience made him a respected figure among his teammates. White's mentorship extended beyond mere technical advice; he was deeply invested in the holistic development of the younger players.

White's leadership approach was characterized by leading by example. His impeccable work ethic set a high standard for the team. He was often the first to arrive for practice and the last to leave, showcasing his dedication and commitment to the sport. This level of discipline and dedication was contagious, inspiring his teammates to elevate their work ethic and approach to the game.

The positive team culture White fostered was pivotal in building team chemistry and unity. He had an innate ability to bring people together, ensuring that every team member, regardless of their role, felt valued and included. His leadership went beyond the usual authoritative style; it was underpinned by empathy and understanding, creating a supportive and cohesive team environment.

White's spiritual leadership was also a significant aspect of his influence. His deep faith was a cornerstone of his life, and he often provided spiritual guidance to his teammates. This spiritual dimension of his leadership provided a source of strength and inspiration for many within the team, transcending the boundaries of the football field.

His respect for diversity and ability to unify players from various backgrounds towards a common goal was remarkable. He fostered an environment of mutual respect and focus on collective success, rather than individual achievements.

Finally, the impact of White's leadership on team performance was undeniable. Teams he was part of were known for their high-level performances, particularly on defense. His ability to elevate the play of those around him was a key factor in the success and consistency of these teams.

Community Involvement

Reggie White's contributions off the field were as significant as his achievements on it. Known for his deep faith and commitment to community service, he was actively involved in various charitable activities, making a lasting impact in the communities he was part of.

White's community involvement was driven by a genuine desire to make a difference. He was particularly focused on youth development, often participating in programs and events aimed at empowering young people. His efforts ranged from mentoring programs to speaking engagements where he shared his experiences and encouraged young people to pursue their dreams while maintaining strong values and work ethics.

In addition to his focus on youth, White was also involved in efforts to help the underprivileged. He participated in and organized numerous charity events, including fundraisers, food drives, and other initiatives aimed at providing assistance to those in need. His charitable work was not just a peripheral activity; it was a central part of his identity and his life's mission.

White's community service extended to his involvement in religious activities. He was an ordained minister and his faith was a guiding force in his life. He used his platform to spread messages of hope, faith, and unity, often ministering to communities and offering spiritual guidance. His commitment to his faith was evident in his actions and the way he lived his life.

Moreover, White's influence in the community served as a role model for his teammates and fans. He showed that being a professional athlete was about more than just sports; it was also about using one's influence and resources for the greater good. He inspired others in the NFL to engage in community service, setting a precedent for how athletes can positively impact society.

Legacy and Impact

Reggie White's legacy and impact on both the sport of football and his community are profound and enduring. In the realm of professional football, he is remembered as one of the greatest defensive players of all time, a player who redefined the role of a defensive lineman with his incredible skill, strength, and athleticism. His records and achievements on the field set new benchmarks for future generations of players, but it was his approach to the game that truly set him apart. White played with a combination of ferocity and integrity, inspiring his teammates and opponents alike with his sportsmanship and respect for the game.

Beyond his statistical achievements, White's impact on football was also cultural. He was a trailblazer for other athletes, particularly African American players, in a sport that was still grappling with issues of diversity and representation. White carried himself with a dignity and grace that transcended the typical stereotypes of professional athletes, and in doing so, he opened doors for others to follow.

Off the field, White's legacy is equally significant. His deep commitment to community service and his faith made him a beloved figure in the communities he was part of. He was not just an athlete who played for a city; he was a member of the community who genuinely cared about the welfare of its people. His charitable work, especially with youth and the underprivileged, had a lasting impact, changing lives and inspiring others to give back.

White's role as a spiritual leader also marked a significant aspect of his legacy. He used his platform to spread messages of faith, hope, and unity, impacting not just those in his immediate community but also reaching a broader audience. His ability to integrate his faith so seamlessly into his public persona was groundbreaking, challenging others in the public eye to be open and authentic about their beliefs and values.

Inspiration from his life

Reggie White's life offers a wealth of inspiration, providing lessons in leadership, the importance of giving back, and the pursuit of excellence that resonate far beyond the football field. His approach to life and sport exemplifies how an individual can make a significant impact through their actions and values.

In terms of leadership, White demonstrated that true leadership is multifaceted. It involves leading by example, mentoring others, showing resilience in the face of adversity, and maintaining integrity. White's dedication to his sport and his team set a high standard for his peers. He showed that a leader is not just someone who excels in their own role but also elevates those around them. His ability to inspire and unite his teammates was pivotal in his teams' successes, proving that effective leadership is as much about building others up as it is about individual achievement.

White's life also underscores the importance of giving back. His extensive community work, especially with youth and underprivileged groups, highlights the role that public figures can play in making a positive difference in society. He used his platform and resources not for personal glorification but to uplift others. This aspect of his legacy teaches the value of compassion and empathy, showing that success is not measured solely by personal achievements but also by the impact one has on the lives of others.

Moreover, White's pursuit of excellence in his professional career sets a benchmark for aspiring athletes and individuals in any field. He approached his craft with a relentless work ethic, a constant desire to improve, and a commitment to maintaining the highest standards. This pursuit was not just about achieving personal goals but also about setting an example for others. His life demonstrates that excellence is a continuous journey, one that requires dedication, discipline, and a willingness to continuously learn and adapt.

In essence, Reggie White's life is a powerful reminder of the impact one individual can have through their approach to leadership, community involvement, and personal excellence. His legacy serves as a guide on how to live a life that is not only successful in a conventional sense but also rich in character and positive influence. His story is a testament to the fact that true greatness involves not just what one achieves for oneself but also what one contributes to the betterment of others.

The Greatest Show on Turf

Formation of the Team

The Greatest Show on Turf, a nickname aptly given to the St. Louis Rams of the late 1990s and early 2000s, was a team that redefined offensive football in the NFL. The formation of this team, which became known for its explosive and dynamic offense, is a story of strategic team-building and the assembly of a unique blend of talent.

The foundation of the Greatest Show on Turf was laid when Dick Vermeil took over as the head coach in 1997. Vermeil began the process of overhauling the Rams' roster, focusing on acquiring players who could fit into a high-powered, innovative offensive system. The coaching staff, including offensive coordinator Mike Martz, played a crucial role in identifying the right players to fit this vision.

One of the most significant moves was the drafting of running back Marshall Faulk from the Indianapolis Colts in 1999. Faulk's versatility as a rusher and receiver made him an ideal fit for the Rams' offensive philosophy. He became a central figure in the team's success, known for his ability to make big plays and his prowess in both the running and passing games.

The emergence of quarterback Kurt Warner in 1999 was a pivotal moment in the formation of the Greatest Show on Turf. Warner, who had been relatively unknown and had spent time in the Arena Football League and NFL Europe, stepped in for the injured Trent Green in the preseason. His incredible performance that season, marked by precise passing and excellent decision-making, was a key factor in the team's transformation.

The Rams also built a strong receiving corps, crucial for their pass-oriented attack. Wide receivers Isaac Bruce and Torry Holt became Warner's primary targets, both known for their speed, route-running skills, and reliable hands. The addition of Az-Zahir Hakim and Ricky Proehl provided depth and versatility to the receiving unit.

The offensive line, often an unsung hero in football, was carefully constructed to provide Warner with the protection he needed to execute the team's aggressive passing game. Anchored by players like Orlando Pace, one of the best offensive tackles in the league, the line was instrumental in both pass protection and run blocking.

On the defensive side, while the Rams were primarily known for their offense, they also put together a competent defense that was good enough to complement their explosive offense. Players like cornerback Aeneas Williams and defensive end Leonard Little contributed to a defense that, while not as celebrated as the offense, played a key role in the team's overall success.

Offensive Strategy

The Greatest Show on Turf was renowned for its innovative offensive strategies that revolutionized the NFL. The core of their offensive philosophy was a high-octane, pass-first approach that emphasized speed, precision, and versatility.

Central to their strategy was the use of the "Air Coryell" offense, adapted and innovated upon by offensive coordinator Mike Martz. This approach relied heavily on stretching the field vertically, thereby creating more space for receivers and exploiting mismatches against slower defenders. The offense was predicated on the idea that any player who caught the ball had the potential to score, making every play a potential game-changer.

Quarterback Kurt Warner was pivotal in executing this strategy. His quick release, accuracy, and ability to read defenses made him the perfect quarterback for this system. Warner's skill in throwing deep balls and his fearlessness in the pocket allowed the Rams to aggressively pursue downfield passes, a hallmark of their offensive strategy.

Running back Marshall Faulk was another key component of the Rams' offensive strategy. He was utilized not just in the traditional running back role but also as a receiver out of the backfield. This dual-threat capability made Faulk an unpredictable and dynamic element in the Rams' offense. His ability to catch passes and create plays in open space was integral to the success of their offensive scheme.

The wide receiver corps, including Isaac Bruce, Torry Holt, Az-Zahir Hakim, and Ricky Proehl, played a crucial role. Their ability to run precise routes and make catches in traffic allowed the Rams to implement a complex and varied passing game. The receivers' speed and agility were critical in beating defensive coverage, and their ability to gain significant yardage after the catch added an extra layer of threat to the offense.

The offensive line's role in this strategy was also critical. Their ability to provide strong pass protection was essential in giving Warner the time needed to execute deep throws. The linemen were also agile and quick, enabling effective run-blocking that was crucial for Faulk's success on the ground and maintaining a balanced offensive attack.

Key Games and Seasons

The 1999 season stands out as a defining moment for the Rams. It was a remarkable turnaround year, where they went from a 4-12 record in the previous season to a Super Bowl-winning team. This season marked the emergence of Kurt Warner as a star quarterback and the team's offense as one of the most potent in NFL history. The Rams finished the regular season with a 13-3 record, topping the NFL in total yards and points scored. The pinnacle of this season was their victory in Super Bowl

XXXIV against the Tennessee Titans, a game that was decided in the final seconds with a dramatic tackle at the one-yard line, preventing a game-tying touchdown.

The 2000 season continued the Rams' offensive dominance, with the team once again leading the NFL in total yards and scoring. Although they fell short in the playoffs, their offensive prowess remained the centerpiece of their success, showcasing their ability to consistently perform at a high level.

The 2001 season saw the Rams returning to the Super Bowl (XXXVI), further solidifying their status as an offensive powerhouse. They finished the regular season with a 14-2 record, once again leading the league in scoring and total yards. The season was marked by memorable performances, including a comeback victory against the San Francisco 49ers where the Rams overcame a 17-point deficit. Although they lost the Super Bowl to the New England Patriots, the season was a testament to their sustained excellence.

Throughout these seasons, several games stand out for their significance. A prime example is a regular-season game against the San Diego Chargers in 2000, where the Rams won 57-31 in a display of offensive fireworks. Another notable game was against the Minnesota Vikings in the 1999 playoffs, where the Rams showcased their explosive offense in a high-scoring and thrilling victory.

Team Dynamics

The team dynamics of the St. Louis Rams during the Greatest Show on Turf era were characterized by a unique synergy between players and coaches, which was foundational to their success. This period showcased a harmonious blend of innovative coaching and exceptional player talent, underpinned by a shared commitment to a high-octane offensive strategy.

At the core of this dynamic was the relationship between head coach Dick Vermeil, offensive coordinator Mike Martz, and the players. Vermeil, known for his emotional coaching style, was adept at motivating his players and building a strong team ethos. His ability to connect with players on a personal level created a sense of family within the team. Martz, on the other hand, was the architect of the Rams' revolutionary offense. His creative play-calling and willingness to take risks were instrumental in unleashing the team's offensive potential.

Quarterback Kurt Warner's role in this dynamic cannot be overstated. His remarkable story from undrafted player to NFL MVP was a source of inspiration for the team. Warner's leadership, both on and off the field, and his exceptional execution of Martz's offense were pivotal. His rapport with his receivers, particularly Isaac Bruce and Torry Holt, was evident in their on-field chemistry. The trust and understanding between Warner and his receivers allowed for precise timing and execution, which was critical in the fast-paced, aggressive passing game.

Running back Marshall Faulk's versatility added another dimension to the team's dynamics. Faulk's ability to contribute both in the running and passing game made him a focal point of the offense and a challenge for opposing defenses. His intelligence and understanding of the game made him an extension of the coaching staff on the field.

The offensive line's cohesion and performance were also key factors in the team's dynamics. Anchored by players like Orlando Pace, the line excelled in both pass protection and run blocking, providing the foundation for the team's explosive offense. Their coordination and ability to work as a unit were critical in giving Warner the time needed to execute plays and Faulk the lanes for rushing.

Defensively, while the Rams were primarily known for their offense, the defensive unit played a complementary role that should not be overlooked. Players like defensive end Leonard Little and cornerback Aeneas Williams contributed to a defense that, while not as celebrated, provided crucial support to the team's overall success.

Impact on NFL

The Greatest Show on Turf had a profound and lasting impact on the NFL, influencing the style of play of numerous other teams and the league as a whole. Their dynamic and high-powered offensive approach marked a significant shift in how football was played and viewed.

One of the most notable impacts was the emphasis on the passing game. The Rams' success with their aggressive, air-centric offense demonstrated the effectiveness of a pass-first strategy, leading to a league-wide trend in favor of more open, high-scoring offensive schemes. Their ability to consistently produce big plays and rack up points quickly shifted the strategic focus for many teams from a balanced run-pass approach to one that heavily favored the passing game.

The Rams also influenced the way teams approached the quarterback position. Kurt Warner's story of rising from obscurity to become a league MVP and Super Bowl champion inspired teams to look beyond traditional routes to find quarterback talent. His quick decision-making, accuracy, and ability to execute complex plays set new standards for quarterbacks. Following the Rams' success, the league saw an increased focus on developing quarterbacks who could perform in high-tempo, pass-heavy offenses.

Wide receiver usage and development also changed as a result of the Rams' success. The effectiveness of Isaac Bruce, Torry Holt, and others in the Rams' system demonstrated the value of having multiple high-quality receivers who could run precise routes and make plays in space. This influenced other teams to invest more in the receiver position, seeking players who could offer similar versatility and impact.

Moreover, the Greatest Show on Turf led to innovations in offensive play-calling and design. Mike Martz's creative and sometimes unconventional playbook encouraged other offensive coordinators to experiment and innovate, pushing the boundaries of traditional NFL offenses. This period saw a significant evolution in offensive strategies, with teams becoming more willing to adopt unorthodox formations and plays.

Defensively, the Rams' style prompted changes in how teams structured their defenses. The need to counteract high-powered offenses like that of the Rams led to a greater emphasis on pass rush and secondary play. Defensive coordinators had to devise new schemes and strategies to slow down or disrupt offenses that were increasingly focused on vertical passing and speed.

Lessons in Teamwork and Innovation

The St. Louis Rams offers valuable lessons in teamwork and innovation, emphasizing the importance of collaboration and the willingness to embrace new approaches in achieving success. This period in NFL history serves as a compelling case study on how collective effort and creative thinking can lead to outstanding results.

Teamwork was a cornerstone of the Rams' success. Their offense, though filled with individual stars like Kurt Warner, Marshall Faulk, Isaac Bruce, and Torry Holt, thrived on the players' ability to work seamlessly together. Each player understood their role and how it contributed to the greater good of the team. This sense of unity and mutual support was crucial in executing their complex, high-speed offense. The offensive line's ability to work in harmony provided Warner with the protection he needed, while the receivers' understanding of their routes and timing allowed for a highly efficient passing game. This level of coordination and cooperation was a testament to the team's emphasis on collective performance over individual accolades.

Innovation was equally pivotal to the Rams' success. Under the guidance of head coach Dick Vermeil and offensive coordinator Mike Martz, the Rams were not afraid to try new and unconventional approaches. Their offensive scheme was a radical departure from the more conservative, run-focused strategies prevalent at the time. Martz's innovative play-calling and the team's adoption of a risk-taking, aggressive style of play disrupted traditional defensive strategies and changed the way offense was played in the NFL. This willingness to innovate and adapt was a key factor in the team's ability to stay ahead of opponents and continually evolve.

The Rams also demonstrated the importance of adaptability and flexibility within their teamwork and innovation. Players were often asked to perform roles or tasks that stretched their traditional skill sets, as seen in Faulk's dual role as a runner and receiver. This flexibility allowed the Rams to be more dynamic and unpredictable, making them harder to defend against.

Furthermore, the team's success underlined the value of having a clear, shared vision. The coaches and players were all aligned in their goal to create a high-powered, efficient offense. This shared vision fostered a strong team culture where innovation was encouraged, and players were motivated to work together towards a common objective.

In essence, the lessons in teamwork and innovation from the Greatest Show on Turf era are invaluable. They highlight how effective collaboration, combined with a willingness to embrace new ideas and approaches, can lead to groundbreaking success. This era of the NFL serves as an inspiration, showing that teamwork and innovation are not just vital for success in sports but are applicable principles in various fields and endeavors.

Jason Witten: The Iron Man

Early Life and Career

Jason Witten, known as "The Iron Man" of the NFL, has a career that is as notable for its longevity and consistency as it is for its excellence. His journey from a small-town boy to one of the most reliable and durable tight ends in NFL history is a story of perseverance, hard work, and natural talent.

Witten's early life in Elizabethton, Tennessee, laid the groundwork for his future success. Born on May 6, 1982, he grew up in a family that loved football, which helped ignite his passion for the game at a young age. His childhood was marked by a strong work ethic, instilled in him by his family, which would become a defining characteristic throughout his career.

In high school, Witten excelled both academically and athletically. He played linebacker and tight end at Elizabethton High School, showcasing his versatility and natural ability on the football field. His performance in high school caught the attention of college scouts, leading to his recruitment by the University of Tennessee. It was here that Witten's potential began to fully take shape.

At the University of Tennessee, Witten transitioned to playing tight end full-time, a move that would define his football career. He quickly made a name for himself, becoming known for his reliable hands, impressive route-running ability, and strong blocking skills. His time at Tennessee was marked by significant growth and development, both on and off the field, setting the stage for his future success in the NFL.

Witten's professional career began when he was drafted by the Dallas Cowboys in the third round of the 2003 NFL Draft. This moment marked the start of what would be an extraordinary career in the league. From the outset, Witten's dedication to the game, his resilience, and his ability to consistently perform at a high level were evident. He quickly became an integral part of the Cowboys' offense, known for his dependability as a receiver and his effectiveness as a blocker.

Consistency and Durability

Jason Witten's NFL career is distinguished not only by his achievements as a tight end but also by his extraordinary consistency and durability. His ability to maintain a high level of performance game after game, year after year, set him apart as one of the most reliable players in the league.

A cornerstone of Witten's career was his remarkable record for consecutive starts. Demonstrating an almost unparalleled level of physical resilience and mental toughness, Witten became a fixture on the field for the Dallas Cowboys. His streak of consecutive starts is a testament to his dedication to maintaining his physical condition, as well as his commitment to being a dependable presence for his team. This consistency was not just a matter of showing up; it was about performing at an elite level every game.

Witten's durability was particularly impressive given the demanding nature of the tight end position, which requires a unique combination of physical strength for blocking and agility for receiving. Throughout his career, he consistently delivered top-notch performances, showcasing his ability to catch passes, run effective routes, and block with prowess. His reliability as a receiver made him a favorite target for Cowboys quarterbacks and a crucial element of the team's offensive strategy.

This consistency extended beyond his physical presence on the field. Witten's knowledge of the game, his understanding of defenses, and his ability to read plays contributed significantly to his ability to perform consistently. His preparation for games was meticulous, studying opponents and understanding their tendencies, which allowed him to adjust his play style as needed.

Witten's durability was also a reflection of his mental fortitude. Playing through injuries and the wear-and-tear of a physically demanding sport, he demonstrated a remarkable ability to focus and deliver under all conditions. This mental toughness, combined with his physical durability, made him an invaluable asset to the Cowboys.

The impact of Witten's consistency and durability can be seen not only in his personal statistics and records but also in the trust and confidence he instilled in his teammates and coaches. Knowing that Witten would be there, game after game, year after year, provided a sense of stability and reliability to the team's offense.

Role as a Tight End

Jason Witten's role as a tight end in the NFL was a defining aspect of his career, showcasing not only his physical and technical abilities but also his understanding of the game. The tight end position is one of the most versatile and demanding roles in football, requiring a unique blend of skills typically associated with both linemen and receivers. Witten excelled in this role, setting a standard for future players at the position.

As a tight end, Witten's responsibilities were multifaceted. He was required to be an effective blocker, both in the running game and in pass protection. His blocking abilities were crucial in creating running lanes for the running backs and providing the necessary time for quarterbacks to execute plays. Witten's strength and technique as a blocker were exemplary, often matching up effectively against larger defensive linemen and linebackers.

In addition to his blocking duties, Witten was also a skilled receiver, known for his reliable hands, route-running abilities, and knack for making crucial catches. His role in the passing game was integral to the Cowboys' offense. He had the versatility to run a variety of routes, from short and intermediate routes to longer downfield passes. His ability to find openings in the defense and make catches in traffic made him a trusted target, particularly in key third-down situations and in the red zone.

Witten's contributions to the tight end position extended beyond the physical aspects of the game. His football intelligence was a critical component of his success. He possessed a deep understanding of offensive schemes and defenses, which allowed him to make quick and smart decisions on the field. This football IQ enabled him to identify and exploit mismatches against opposing defenses, contributing significantly to his team's strategic approach.

Witten's durability and consistency also played a vital role in his contributions as a tight end. His ability to stay healthy and perform at a high level week after week provided the Cowboys with a reliable option in both the passing and running games. This dependability was a key factor in the longevity and success of his career.

Furthermore, Witten's leadership as a tight end was invaluable. He was a mentor to younger players and a role model in how to approach the game professionally. His work ethic and dedication to improving his skills were qualities that inspired his teammates and set a positive example within the locker room.

Leadership and Mentorship

Jason Witten's role as a leader and mentor on his team was as integral to his legacy as his on-field achievements. Throughout his illustrious career, Witten demonstrated exemplary leadership qualities, both in the locker room and on the field, earning the respect and admiration of teammates, coaches, and opponents alike.

Witten's leadership style was grounded in leading by example. He was known for his tireless work ethic, consistently being one of the first players to arrive at practice and the last to leave. This dedication to his craft set a standard for his teammates, showcasing the level of commitment required to excel in the NFL. His approach to the game, marked by a relentless pursuit of improvement and perfection, served as a blueprint for younger players.

Beyond setting an example with his work ethic, Witten was also a vocal leader. He was not hesitant to speak up in team meetings or on the field, providing guidance and motivation. His years of experience and deep understanding of the game made his insights invaluable, especially to the younger members of the team. Witten had a unique ability to communicate effectively with players of all backgrounds and experience levels, making him a unifying figure within the team.

As a mentor, Witten was always available to his teammates, offering advice on everything from game techniques to handling the pressures of professional football. He took a particular interest in the development of younger players, understanding the challenges they faced and offering his support to help them navigate their careers. His willingness to share his knowledge and experiences made him a cherished figure among his peers.

Witten's leadership extended beyond on-field performance. He was a role model in terms of professionalism and character. He handled himself with grace and integrity, demonstrating how to balance the demands of a high-profile athletic career with personal and family life. This aspect of his leadership was particularly impactful, as it showed his teammates the importance of character and integrity in building a successful career.

Moreover, Witten's presence in the locker room was a stabilizing force. In times of adversity, his calm and positive demeanor helped to maintain team morale. His ability to keep the team focused and motivated, especially during challenging times, was a testament to his leadership qualities.

Off-Field Contributions

Jason's impact extended well beyond the football field, with his off-field contributions and charitable work reflecting his commitment to the community. Known for his generosity and compassion, Witten dedicated much of his time and resources to various philanthropic efforts, making a significant difference in the lives of many.

One of the key areas of Witten's community involvement was his focus on family violence prevention. Inspired by his personal experiences, Witten established the Jason Witten SCORE Foundation, which aimed to provide support and assistance to families affected by domestic violence. The foundation's initiatives included education and prevention programs, as well as the establishment of emergency shelters and support services for victims. His dedication to this cause was driven by a deep understanding of the impact of family violence and a commitment to helping those in need.

Witten was also actively involved in youth development programs. He recognized the importance of positive role models and guidance for young people, particularly those in underserved communities. Through various camps and educational programs, he sought to inspire and motivate children and adolescents, teaching them the values of hard work, perseverance, and integrity. His engagement with youth extended beyond just sports, as he often spoke about the importance of education, good character, and making positive life choices.

His charitable efforts included partnerships with numerous organizations dedicated to improving the lives of individuals and communities. Witten was often seen participating in fundraising events, charity matches, and public awareness campaigns, using his platform as a professional athlete to draw attention to important social issues.

Additionally, Witten's involvement in the community was characterized by his approachability and genuine desire to connect with people. He frequently made appearances at schools, hospitals, and community events, where he interacted with fans and community members, lending his support and bringing smiles to many faces.

Career Lessons

Jason Witten's illustrious career in the NFL offers numerous valuable lessons, with his resilience, reliability, and strong work ethic standing out as key attributes that any aspiring athlete or professional can aspire to emulate. These qualities not only defined his success on the field but also shaped his character and reputation off it.

Resilience was a hallmark of Witten's career. In the demanding and physically taxing world of professional football, he faced numerous challenges, including injuries and the inevitable ups and downs of team performance. Yet, Witten consistently demonstrated an ability to bounce back, whether from personal setbacks or team losses. His resilience was evident in his approach to recovery and preparation, always working diligently to return to the field in top form. This resilience extended to his mental toughness, maintaining focus and a positive attitude even under pressure.

Reliability was another key aspect of Witten's career. In a sport where consistency can be as valuable as talent, Witten was a model of dependability. His record for consecutive starts is a testament to this reliability, as is his reputation as a player who could always be counted on to make the crucial catch or block. His teammates and coaches knew they could rely on him to perform his duties to the best of his ability every game, making him an invaluable member of the Dallas Cowboys.

A strong work ethic was the foundation upon which Witten built his career. He was known for his dedication to training, continually working to improve his skills and understanding of the game. His commitment extended beyond physical training to include studying game film, understanding opponent strategies, and staying abreast of changes in the game. Witten's work ethic set a standard for his teammates and made him a role model for young players.

The career lessons from Jason Witten's journey in the NFL are manifold. His resilience teaches the importance of facing challenges head-on and using them as opportunities for growth. His reliability underscores the value of consistency and the trust it builds within a team. His strong work ethic highlights the dedication required to excel and the importance of continuous self-improvement. These qualities not only made Witten one of the most respected players in the NFL but also serve as guiding principles for success in any endeavor.

Vince Lombardi's Leadership

Early Life & Career

Vince Lombardi's journey to becoming one of the most iconic figures in the history of American football is a story of determination, passion, and an unwavering commitment to excellence. His early life and the path that led him to a legendary coaching career provide insight into the development of his leadership style, which would later revolutionize the sport.

Born on June 11, 1913, in Brooklyn, New York, Vince Lombardi grew up in a close-knit Italian-American family. His early life was marked by a strong Catholic faith, a characteristic that would remain significant throughout his life. Lombardi's interest in football began at a young age, and he played the sport at St. Francis Preparatory School, where his talents on the field started to emerge. This early exposure to football was the beginning of a lifelong passion for the game.

Following high school, Lombardi attended Fordham University in the Bronx, where he became a key member of their football team, known as the "Seven Blocks of Granite." His time at Fordham was instrumental in shaping his understanding of the game and his approach to teamwork and discipline. Lombardi's experience at Fordham, both academically and athletically, laid the groundwork for his future coaching philosophies.

After his college career, Lombardi embarked on a path that would lead him toward coaching. His initial foray into a professional career was not in football but as a high school teacher, where he also coached various sports, including football, basketball, and baseball. This experience in teaching and coaching at the high school level was crucial in developing his skills in leadership and mentoring young athletes.

Lombardi's break into collegiate and professional football coaching came after several years in high school coaching. He served as an assistant coach at Fordham and later at the United States Military Academy at West Point. His time at West Point, under the mentorship of Colonel Red Blaik, was particularly influential. Blaik's emphasis on discipline, attention to detail, and rigorous standards deeply resonated with Lombardi and would become hallmarks of his own coaching style.

Lombardi's transition to the National Football League (NFL) began with assistant coaching positions, first with the New York Giants, where he served as the offensive coordinator. His success with the Giants, particularly in developing a potent offensive strategy, caught the attention of the NFL and set the stage for his future success as a head coach.

Coaching Philosophy

Vince Lombardi's coaching philosophy was a unique blend of discipline, hard work, and an unwavering commitment to excellence, principles that not only shaped his approach to football but also left a lasting impact on the sport. His philosophy extended beyond the X's and O's of the game, delving into the character and motivation of his players, making him one of the most revered coaches in NFL history.

Central to Lombardi's coaching ethos was the concept of discipline. He believed that discipline was the foundation of success, both on and off the field. This was evident in the way he ran his practices and organized his team. Lombardi's practices were meticulously planned and executed with precision. He expected his players to give their best effort at all times, and he had little tolerance for mistakes or lack of effort. This disciplined approach extended to all aspects of the team's operations, from training routines to game strategies.

Lombardi's philosophy also emphasized the value of hard work. He was a firm believer that success was not a matter of talent alone, but the result of relentless effort and continuous improvement. He instilled this mindset in his players, pushing them to their limits to bring out their best. Lombardi's famous quote, "The only place success comes before work is in the dictionary," encapsulates his belief in the primacy of hard work.

Another key aspect of Lombardi's coaching was his focus on teamwork and collective success. He consistently emphasized the importance of each player's role in the team's achievements. Lombardi fostered a sense of unity and camaraderie among his players, believing that a cohesive team was stronger than the sum of its individual parts. His ability to create a team-first mentality was crucial in building a winning culture.

Leadership was at the heart of Lombardi's coaching philosophy. He led by example, demonstrating dedication, integrity, and a relentless pursuit of excellence. Lombardi's leadership style was both authoritative and empathetic. He was known for his fiery speeches and motivational tactics, but he also cared deeply for his players, understanding their individual needs and challenges. He was a master at motivating his players, finding the right words and actions to inspire peak performance.

Lombardi's approach to coaching and leadership also involved a deep understanding of the game's strategic aspects. He was an innovative thinker, always looking for ways to gain a competitive edge. His teams were well-prepared and adaptable, capable of adjusting their strategies to meet the challenges of each game.

Success with the Green Bay Packers

Vince Lombardi's tenure with the Green Bay Packers is celebrated as one of the most successful periods in NFL history, particularly highlighted by his team's victories in the first two Super Bowls. Under Lombardi's leadership, the Packers transformed into a dominant force in football, setting new standards for success and excellence.

When Lombardi took over as head coach in 1959, the Packers were struggling, but he quickly turned the team around. His first season marked a significant improvement, laying the foundation for the successes to come. Lombardi's impact on the Packers was immediate and profound, instilling a winning mentality and reshaping the team's culture and strategy.

The pinnacle of Lombardi's success with the Packers came in the 1966 and 1967 seasons, culminating in victories in Super Bowl I and II. These historic wins not only solidified Lombardi's legacy but also marked a significant moment in the history of the sport, as the Super Bowl would become the pinnacle of success in professional football.

Super Bowl I, played on January 15, 1967, saw the Packers defeat the Kansas City Chiefs with a commanding score of 35-10. Lombardi's strategic acumen was on full display during the game, with the Packers showcasing their superior preparation and execution. The victory was a testament to Lombardi's effective coaching and his ability to get the best out of his players in high-stakes situations.

The following year, in Super Bowl II, the Packers faced the Oakland Raiders and secured a consecutive championship with a 33-14 victory. This game further demonstrated Lombardi's excellence in coaching, as the Packers outplayed the Raiders with a balanced attack on offense and a stifling defense. Lombardi's leadership and game planning were crucial in guiding the Packers to their second straight Super Bowl win.

Lombardi's achievements with the Packers extended beyond these Super Bowl victories. He led the team to multiple NFL Championships prior to the Super Bowl era, cementing their status as a dynasty. The team's consistent performance under his guidance, characterized by strategic brilliance, discipline, and an unmatched work ethic, made them the team of the decade.

Lombardi's time with the Green Bay Packers also left an indelible mark on the team's identity. The principles of teamwork, perseverance, and the relentless pursuit of excellence became ingrained in the Packers' ethos, a legacy that persists to this day. The Packers' stadium, Lambeau Field, became a symbol of this legacy, often referred to as the "frozen tundra," where Lombardi's teams showcased their toughness and determination.

Work Ethic and Discipline

Vince Lombardi's legendary work ethic and his emphasis on discipline were foundational elements of his coaching philosophy and key factors in the success of the Green Bay Packers during his tenure. Lombardi's approach to these aspects not only shaped his teams but also left a lasting legacy in the realm of professional sports.

Lombardi's work ethic was unparalleled. He was known for his meticulous preparation, often working long hours studying game film, developing strategies, and planning practices. His commitment to understanding every facet of the game and his relentless pursuit of perfection were infectious. Lombardi believed that there were no shortcuts to success, and this belief was evident in the way he approached his coaching duties. He expected the same level of commitment from his players and staff, creating an environment where hard work was the norm.

Discipline was a cornerstone of Lombardi's coaching style. He ran his practices with military precision, demanding punctuality, focus, and full effort from every player. Lombardi's practices were intense and purposeful, designed to maximize efficiency and prepare his team for any game situation. He had an unwavering expectation that his players would give their all, both on the practice field and during games.

Lombardi instilled discipline in his players by holding them to high standards and ensuring accountability. He believed that discipline was not just about following rules but about self-control, responsibility, and mutual respect. Lombardi's players knew that meeting these standards was essential for their individual and the team's success. This discipline extended beyond the field, as Lombardi expected his players to conduct themselves with integrity and professionalism in all aspects of their lives.

The discipline Lombardi instilled was not achieved through fear or intimidation but rather through respect and motivation. He had a unique ability to connect with his players, understanding their strengths and weaknesses. Lombardi used this understanding to motivate them, pushing them to reach their full potential. His discipline was balanced with a genuine care for his players, which helped him build strong, trusting relationships with them.

Moreover, Lombardi's work ethic and discipline extended to his approach to teamwork and collective effort. He emphasized the importance of each player's role in the team's success and the need for every member to adhere to the team's disciplined approach. This collective discipline was a key factor in the Packers' ability to function as a cohesive and effective unit.

Legacy

Vince's legacy in the NFL is profound and enduring, transcending the era in which he coached and continuing to influence the sport today. His impact goes beyond the numerous championships and records; it is embedded in the culture and ethos of American football. The significance of the Lombardi Trophy, awarded to the Super Bowl winner each year, is a testament to his lasting influence and the respect he commands in the sport.

Lombardi's legacy in the NFL is marked by his revolutionary approach to the game. He transformed the way football was played and coached, emphasizing precision, discipline, and a strong work ethic. His philosophies about leadership, teamwork, and commitment to excellence reshaped the standards for success in the league. Lombardi's impact was such that he became synonymous with winning and excellence, qualities that every team in the NFL aspires to emulate.

The Lombardi Trophy, named in his honor after his death in 1970, symbolizes the pinnacle of success in the NFL. It is not just a trophy but a representation of the ideals Lombardi stood for – excellence, perseverance, and the relentless pursuit of victory. Winning the Lombardi Trophy is the ultimate goal for every NFL team, a powerful motivator that drives players and coaches alike. The trophy's association with Lombardi elevates its significance, making it a coveted prize that symbolizes the highest achievement in professional football.

Lombardi's influence extends beyond strategies and game plans. His philosophies on leadership and character development have become integral to the culture of the NFL. He believed that the principles of success on the football field – discipline, hard work, and dedication – are applicable to all areas of life. This holistic approach to coaching and leadership has inspired countless players, coaches, and fans, leaving a legacy that goes beyond the sport.

Moreover, Lombardi's emphasis on equality and inclusivity, particularly during a time of significant social change in the United States, contributed to his lasting legacy. He was a proponent of meritocracy, judging players and coaches solely on their abilities and contributions to the team, regardless of their race or background. This stance not only had a profound impact on his players but also influenced the attitudes within the broader NFL community.

Leadership Lessons

Vince Lombardi's career offers a wealth of leadership lessons that extend far beyond the realm of football, providing valuable insights into team management and effective leadership. His approach and philosophies have been studied and emulated by leaders in various fields, reflecting the universal applicability of his principles.

One of the key lessons from Lombardi's career is the importance of a clear vision and goals. Lombardi was successful in part because he had a clear vision of what he wanted his teams to achieve and communicated these goals effectively. He instilled a sense of purpose in his players, making sure everyone understood the team's objectives and their role in achieving them. This clarity of purpose was crucial in driving the team towards collective success.

Lombardi also taught the value of discipline and hard work. He believed that success was not attainable without a strong work ethic and adherence to discipline. This principle was not only about following rules but also about self-discipline, commitment to one's role, and the consistent effort to perform at one's best. Lombardi's insistence on discipline created a structured and focused environment conducive to high performance.

Another significant lesson from Lombardi's leadership is the power of motivation and inspiration. Lombardi knew how to motivate his players, often pushing them beyond what they thought was possible. He was adept at understanding each player's motivators and used this knowledge to get the best out of his team. His motivational skills were complemented by his ability to inspire through his own passion and dedication to the game.

Lombardi's approach to teamwork and collaboration was another key aspect of his leadership philosophy. He emphasized the concept of the team over the individual, fostering a culture where collective success was valued above personal accolades. Lombardi believed that every member of the team had a vital role to play, no matter how small it seemed. This inclusive approach not only enhanced team cohesion but also encouraged each player to contribute their best for the common goal.

Effective communication was a hallmark of Lombardi's leadership style. He was known for his ability to clearly articulate his thoughts and strategies, ensuring that every team member understood their responsibilities. His communication was direct and often demanding, but it was also underpinned by a sense of trust and respect for his players. Lombardi's open and honest communication fostered a transparent environment where feedback was valued and used for continuous improvement.

Lombardi also exemplified resilience and the ability to adapt. In the face of challenges, whether on the field or off, he displayed a remarkable capacity to persevere and adapt his strategies as needed. This resilience inspired his team to face adversity head-on and turn challenges into opportunities for growth.

Finally, Lombardi's leadership was characterized by his integrity and commitment to ethical principles. He led with a strong moral compass, emphasizing the importance of doing things the right way. His commitment to fairness and equality, especially during a time of social change, demonstrated his understanding that true leadership extends beyond the confines of the sport.

Doug Williams: Breaking Barriers

Early Years and College Career

Doug Williams' journey to becoming a trailblazer in professional football is a story of talent, determination, and breaking barriers. His early years and college career laid the foundation for his groundbreaking achievements in the NFL.

Williams was born on August 9, 1955, in Zachary, Louisiana. Growing up in the segregated South, he faced numerous challenges and obstacles, but his passion for football shone through from a young age. His talent was evident during his high school years, where he excelled as a quarterback, displaying a powerful arm and a keen understanding of the game.

Williams' college career at Grambling State University under the legendary coach Eddie Robinson further showcased his skills and potential. At Grambling, a historically Black university renowned for its football program, Williams thrived, honing his abilities as a quarterback. He led the team to three Southwestern Athletic Conference Championships, earning accolades for his strong arm, accuracy, and leadership on the field.

During his time at Grambling, Williams set several school records and was recognized as a top college quarterback. His impressive performances drew the attention of NFL scouts, despite the prevailing biases against African American quarterbacks at the time. Williams' success in college was not just a testament to his athletic abilities but also a challenge to the stereotypes and barriers that existed in football.

Williams' college career was marked by significant achievements, including being named a Black College All-American and finishing fourth in the Heisman Trophy voting in 1977. These accomplishments underscored his readiness for the professional stage and set the scene for his pioneering career in the NFL.

Challenges in the NFL

Doug Williams' entry into the NFL was marked by significant challenges, particularly the racial barriers that existed regarding African American quarterbacks. His journey in the league highlighted both his resilience in the face of adversity and the broader struggle for racial equality in professional sports.

When Williams was drafted by the Tampa Bay Buccaneers in 1978, he became the first African American quarterback to be drafted in the first round. This groundbreaking moment was a step forward, but it also brought with it a set of challenges unique to his pioneering role. At the time, there were prevailing biases and stereotypes about the ability of African American players to lead as quarterbacks. Williams had to not only prove himself as a skilled player but also confront and disprove these deeply entrenched racial stereotypes.

Williams faced scrutiny and skepticism from some fans, media, and even within the league, much of it rooted in racial prejudice. Despite his college success, there were doubts about his ability to perform at the NFL level. This skepticism was often more intense than that faced by his white counterparts, placing an additional burden on him to perform.

Financial disparities also marked Williams' experience in the NFL. Despite being a starting quarterback, he was among the lowest-paid in the league, reflecting broader issues of racial inequality in pay and treatment. Williams' contract negotiations with the Buccaneers were particularly contentious and highlighted the racial inequities prevalent in the league.

Despite these challenges, Williams' performance on the field was commendable. He led the Buccaneers to three playoff appearances and one NFC Championship game, demonstrating his leadership and skill as a quarterback. His ability to maintain focus and excel under pressure was a testament to his mental toughness and character.

Williams' time with the Buccaneers eventually came to an end, partly due to the unresolved contract disputes. He spent time playing in the United States Football League (USFL) before returning to the NFL with the Washington Redskins. His career trajectory was a reflection of the ongoing struggles faced by African American players in the league, especially those in quarterback roles.

Super Bowl XXII

Super Bowl XXII was a defining moment in Doug Williams' career and a significant milestone in the history of the NFL. His performance in this game not only cemented his status as an elite quarterback but also marked a groundbreaking achievement as he became the first African American quarterback to win a Super Bowl.

The game, played on January 31, 1988, saw Williams' Washington Redskins face off against the Denver Broncos. The beginning of the game was challenging for Williams and the Redskins, as they quickly fell behind. However, what unfolded thereafter was nothing short of remarkable. Williams, displaying resilience and exceptional skill, led a stunning turnaround.

In one of the most memorable performances in Super Bowl history, Williams threw for 340 yards and four touchdowns. His explosive second quarter, where he threw four touchdown passes, turned the game on its head and set several Super Bowl records. It was a showcase of his arm strength, accuracy, and ability to read the defense. Williams' performance was even more impressive considering he had suffered a minor injury earlier in the game, demonstrating his toughness and commitment.

The significance of Williams' achievement in leading his team to a 42-10 victory went far beyond the game itself. As the first African American quarterback to start and win a Super Bowl, he shattered a significant racial barrier in the sport. His success challenged the stereotypes and biases surrounding African American quarterbacks and proved that talent and leadership know no racial bounds.

Williams' victory in Super Bowl XXII was a source of inspiration for countless aspiring African American athletes. It represented a moment of progress in the ongoing struggle for racial equality in sports and beyond. His triumph was not just celebrated by the Redskins and their fans but also by the wider African American community and supporters of equality across the nation.

The impact of Williams' achievement was also felt in the NFL, as it opened doors for future generations of African American quarterbacks. His success laid the groundwork for other talented quarterbacks of color who would follow in his footsteps, changing the face of the quarterback position in the league.

Overcoming Racism

Doug Williams' journey in the NFL was marked by his resilience and fortitude in the face of racial prejudice. His experiences and responses to the challenges he faced offer a compelling narrative about overcoming racism in a professional landscape that was often unwelcoming to African American quarterbacks.

Throughout his career, Williams encountered various forms of racial prejudice, from stereotyping about the capabilities of African American quarterbacks to facing disparities in treatment and pay. He confronted these challenges with a calm and determined demeanor, choosing to let his performance on the field speak for itself. Williams' ability to perform at a high level, especially under intense scrutiny and pressure, was a direct rebuke to the stereotypes and biases that sought to undermine his capabilities.

Williams' approach to dealing with racism was characterized by a focus on his own goals and aspirations, rather than the negativity and discrimination he faced. He maintained a professional attitude, showing that his talent and work ethic were the defining aspects of his career, not the color of his skin. This approach not only helped him navigate a challenging professional environment but also served as an inspiration for other African American players.

His triumph in Super Bowl XXII was a pivotal moment in challenging racial barriers in the NFL. By becoming the first African American quarterback to win a Super Bowl, Williams disproved the pervasive myths about the limitations of black athletes in leadership and high-pressure roles. His success on football's biggest stage sent a powerful message about equality and the potential for excellence regardless of race.

Off the field, Williams was an advocate for equality and inclusivity in sports. He often spoke about his experiences and the need for progress in the treatment of minority athletes. His voice added an important perspective to the conversations about race in sports and helped to raise awareness about the ongoing struggles for racial equality.

Furthermore, Williams' legacy in overcoming racism extends beyond his personal achievements. His success paved the way for future generations of African American quarterbacks, creating opportunities for them to be evaluated on their merits rather than racial stereotypes. His career served as a beacon of hope and a source of motivation for young athletes facing similar challenges.

Legacy and Impact

Doug Williams' legacy and impact on the NFL, particularly regarding the path of African American quarterbacks, is profound and far-reaching. His success and perseverance in the face of adversity have not only carved a place for him in the annals of football history but also opened doors for future generations of players, serving as a source of inspiration and a beacon of change.

Williams' triumph in Super Bowl XXII fundamentally altered perceptions about the capabilities of African American quarterbacks. By excelling in a role that had traditionally been limited to white players, Williams shattered longstanding racial stereotypes within the NFL. His victory was a powerful statement that talent and leadership in the quarterback position are not defined by race. This breakthrough was a significant step forward in the ongoing journey toward racial equality in professional football.

The impact of Williams' career extends beyond his achievements on the field. He laid the groundwork for future African American quarterbacks, setting a precedent that has inspired countless young athletes. His success challenged NFL teams and scouts to reconsider biases in their evaluation and selection of quarterbacks, leading to greater opportunities for black athletes in this pivotal role.

Moreover, Williams' story of perseverance in the face of discrimination and his ultimate triumph have made him an enduring symbol of resilience and determination. His journey resonates with athletes of all backgrounds, particularly those who face similar barriers and biases. Williams' example shows that with talent, hard work, and perseverance, it is possible to overcome challenges and achieve great success.

In the years following Williams' Super Bowl win, there has been a noticeable increase in the number of African American quarterbacks in the NFL. Players like Patrick Mahomes, Lamar Jackson, and Russell Wilson, among others, have risen to prominence, showcasing their skills and leadership. While the journey towards full equality in sports continues, the progress made can be attributed in part to the path Williams paved.

His legacy also extends to his work off the field, where he has been involved in mentoring young players and contributing to their growth and development. Through his actions and his words, Williams continues to inspire and guide future generations, emphasizing the importance of integrity, hard work, and resilience.

Doug Williams' legacy in the NFL is one of groundbreaking achievement and enduring impact. He not only changed the game for African American quarterbacks but also influenced the broader narrative around race and sports. His success serves as a source of inspiration for future generations, reminding them of the power of perseverance and the possibility of transcending barriers to achieve greatness.

The 12th Man

Origin of the 12th Man

The '12th Man' concept, particularly associated with the Seattle Seahawks, is a unique and celebrated tradition in the NFL, symbolizing the powerful impact and support of the team's fans. The origin and history of the 12th Man with the Seahawks reflect the deep connection and interaction between the team and its passionate fan base.

The term '12th Man' is used to represent the fans' role in supporting the eleven players on the field. While the term itself has been used in football for many years, its association with the Seattle Seahawks began to take on a special significance in the early 1980s. The Seahawks' fans, known for their enthusiastic and loud support during games, have created an atmosphere in their home stadium that is renowned for being one of the most intimidating for visiting teams in the NFL.

The Seahawks officially embraced the 12th Man concept in 1984. Understanding the impact that the raucous home crowd was having on the games, the Seahawks' management decided to retire the number 12 jersey as a tribute to their fans. This gesture was a formal acknowledgment of the fans' role as an integral part of the team, symbolically elevating them to the status of an extra player who contributes to the team's performance.

The tradition of the 12th Man took on a physical representation with the raising of the '12th Man Flag' at the Seahawks' home games. Before each home game, a flag with the number 12 is hoisted in the stadium, a ritual that has become a beloved part of the pre-game festivities. This flag-raising is often performed by a past player, local celebrity, or a fan, further symbolizing the unity between the team and its supporters.

The impact of the 12th Man on the Seahawks' games, particularly at their home stadium, Lumen Field (formerly known as CenturyLink Field and Qwest Field), is tangible. The noise generated by the fans has been credited with causing numerous false start penalties and communication issues for opposing teams. The stadium's design, which amplifies the sound, coupled with the fans' enthusiasm, creates an environment that gives the Seahawks a distinct home-field advantage.

Fan Culture and Support

Seattle's fans are renowned for their enthusiastic and spirited support, often cited as some of the loudest and most dedicated in the NFL. This fervor is evident not only in the stadium on game days but throughout the city and region. On game days, Lumen Field becomes a sea of blue and green, with fans donning team colors and participating in spirited chants and cheers. This color coordination and collective cheering create a unified atmosphere that energizes the team and intimidates opponents.

The 12th Man culture extends beyond just cheering during the games. It encompasses a range of traditions and activities that engage the fan community. Tailgating events, fan rallies, and community gatherings are commonplace, fostering a sense of belonging and camaraderie among the supporters. Fans take pride in their role as the 12th Man, viewing their support as a crucial component of the team's success.

The impact of the fan culture on the team is palpable. The noise level in Lumen Field, amplified by the stadium's design, creates an intimidating environment for visiting teams. The fans' noise has led to a measurable impact on the game, contributing to false starts and communication difficulties for the opposition. The Seahawks players and coaches have frequently acknowledged the fans' role in their success, citing the energy and atmosphere they create as a motivating factor.

Seattle's fan culture is also characterized by its longevity and consistency. Even in seasons when the team has not performed as well, the fans' support remains steadfast. This loyalty is a testament to the deep connection between the city and its football team. The fans' commitment goes beyond the typical fair-weather support seen in some sports; it is a year-round, unwavering dedication.

Impact on Games

The impact of fans' presence on sports games is profound and often serves as a critical factor in the outcome of these events. The energy, noise, and enthusiasm of the crowd can significantly influence the performance of athletes and the overall dynamics of a game. There are numerous examples where fan presence has positively impacted games, turning the tide in favor of the home team or creating memorable moments in sports history.

One classic example of fan impact is the concept of the 'home-field advantage' in football. Teams playing in their home stadium often perform better, spurred on by the support of their local fans. This advantage is not just psychological; the noise created by the home crowd can disrupt the visiting team's communication, leading to errors or misplays. For instance, in NFL games, especially in stadiums known for their loud crowds like the Seattle Seahawks' Lumen Field, there have been numerous instances where the home team benefits from false start penalties against the visitors, directly attributable to the noisy environment created by the fans.

In basketball, the influence of a passionate home crowd is evident in pivotal moments during the game. When the home team is trailing, a surge of energy from the crowd following a key play, such as a dunk or a three-pointer, can ignite a comeback. This phenomenon was famously observed during the Chicago Bulls' dynasty in the 1990s, where the electrifying atmosphere at the United Center would often provide the team with a tangible lift, particularly in crucial playoff games.

In soccer, the impact of fans is similarly significant. The atmosphere in stadiums, particularly during important matches like derbies or championship games, can elevate the players' performance. For example, Liverpool Football Club's home ground, Anfield, is renowned for its '12th man' effect, especially during European nights. The supporters' singing of "You'll Never Walk Alone" has become a legendary example of how fan support can inspire players, contributing to the team's impressive record in European competitions.

Baseball also provides instances of fan impact. The roar of the crowd following a home run or a key strikeout can shift the momentum of the game. In the World Series games, where the stakes are highest, home teams often benefit from the energy and encouragement of their fans, helping pitchers perform better and batters to find that extra focus needed in critical at-bats.

Even in individual sports like tennis, athletes often acknowledge the role of the crowd in boosting their performance. Cheering and encouragement from the spectators can provide players with an extra burst of energy and motivation, particularly during long and grueling matches.

Community Involvement

The engagement between the Seattle Seahawks, their fans, and the local community is a dynamic and multifaceted relationship that extends far beyond the football field. Both the team and its passionate fan base are actively involved in various community initiatives, demonstrating a commitment to making a positive impact in the Seattle area.

The Seahawks organization has a strong tradition of community service and outreach. The team runs numerous programs aimed at giving back to the local community, including youth development initiatives, health and wellness campaigns, and educational support activities. These programs often involve players, coaches, and staff members interacting directly with community members, providing mentorship, support, and inspiration.

One notable aspect of the Seahawks' community involvement is their focus on youth empowerment. The team organizes camps, workshops, and clinics that provide young people with opportunities to develop their skills, both in football and in other areas of life. These events are often led by Seahawks players who serve as role models, offering guidance and encouragement to the next generation.

In addition to youth-focused initiatives, the Seahawks are also involved in charitable efforts that address broader community needs. This includes partnerships with local charities and non-profit organizations to support causes such as homelessness, food insecurity, and health care. The team's players and staff often participate in fundraising events, charity matches, and community drives, using their platform to raise awareness and resources for these important issues.

The Seahawks' fan base, known as the 12th Man, also plays a significant role in community engagement. Fans organize and participate in various charitable activities, exemplifying the spirit of community service. From organizing food drives to participating in charity runs and community clean-up events, the fans demonstrate a commitment to supporting and improving their local community.

Moreover, the Seahawks' community involvement extends to times of crisis. The team and its fans have been known to mobilize in response to local and national emergencies, providing aid and support where needed. This responsiveness highlights the organization's role as a community leader and a source of support beyond the realm of sports.

Power of Support

The power of community and fan support in sports is immense, playing a crucial role in not only enhancing the game-day experience but also in contributing to the overall success and vitality of sports teams. This support transcends the physical boundaries of the stadium, creating a deep and enduring connection between the team and its fans.

At its core, community and fan support provides an emotional boost to athletes, often serving as a critical source of motivation and energy. Players frequently draw inspiration from the passion and enthusiasm of their fans, which can elevate their performance levels, particularly in high-stakes or challenging situations. The concept of the 'home advantage' in sports is largely attributed to the support and energy provided by the home fans, showcasing the tangible impact of fan presence on team performance.

Beyond the immediate impact on games, fan support is instrumental in building a team's identity and legacy. Fans contribute to the creation of a unique culture and atmosphere around a team, often characterized by traditions, rituals, and a shared history. This cultural aspect fosters a deeper emotional connection between the team and its supporters, creating a sense of belonging and community that extends beyond the realm of sports.

Fan and community support also plays a vital role in the sustainability and financial health of sports organizations. Ticket sales, merchandise purchases, and fan engagement are crucial economic drivers for teams, enabling them to invest in player development, facilities, and community outreach initiatives. In this way, fans contribute not only to the success of the team on the field but also to its broader operational and financial stability.

Moreover, community and fan involvement in sports can have a significant social impact. Through their collective support for a team, fans from diverse backgrounds come together, fostering a sense of unity and breaking down social barriers. Sports teams often become symbols of local pride and community spirit, especially in times of collective achievement or adversity.

The importance of fan support extends into the development of future athletes as well. In youth sports, encouragement from the community and fans can positively influence young players' development, building their confidence, sportsmanship, and love for the game. This nurturing environment is essential for developing future talent and fostering a lifelong passion for sports.

Lessons in Team and Community Spirit

The 12th Man phenomenon associated with the Seattle Seahawks provides insightful lessons on team and community spirit, reflecting broader themes of unity, support, and the powerful impact of collective action. This unique manifestation of fan engagement offers valuable insights into how communal spirit can elevate a team's performance and foster a deep sense of belonging and pride.

One of the key lessons from the 12th Man is the concept of unity and collective strength. The fans, though not physically on the field, play a crucial role in the team's dynamics, often considered as an extra player due to their impact on the game's atmosphere. This unity demonstrates how a group of individuals, united by a common passion, can contribute significantly to a collective goal. It highlights the strength that comes from solidarity and the shared commitment to support and uplift one another.

The 12th Man also exemplifies the importance of creating an inclusive and welcoming community. The Seahawks' fans come from diverse backgrounds, yet on game day, they come together as one. This inclusive atmosphere fosters a sense of belonging among the fans, reinforcing the idea that each individual, regardless of their background, is an integral part of the community. It's a powerful reminder of how sports can bridge differences and bring people together for a common cause.

Another lesson from the 12th Man is the impact of passionate support and positive reinforcement. The energy and enthusiasm of the fans have a tangible effect on the team's performance, showcasing how encouragement and belief can inspire people to exceed expectations and overcome challenges. This lesson is applicable beyond sports, emphasizing the importance of support and positive reinforcement in any team or community setting.

The 12th Man also teaches the value of resilience and unwavering support. Seahawks fans are known for their steadfast loyalty, supporting the team through both victories and defeats. This unwavering support, even in tough times, exemplifies the strength of character and the importance of standing by each other, fostering a resilient community spirit.

Furthermore, the 12th Man reflects the significance of active participation and engagement in community life. The fans' active involvement in game days and community events underscores the importance of being an engaged and contributing member of a community. It shows that active participation can enrich the community experience, creating a more vibrant and dynamic environment.

The Miracle at the Super Bowl

Background of Super Bowl LI

The Miracle at the Super Bowl, referring to the remarkable events of Super Bowl LI, stands as one of the most memorable moments in NFL history. This game, played on February 5, 2017, at NRG Stadium in Houston, Texas, was a clash between the New England Patriots and the Atlanta Falcons, each bringing their own unique story to this championship showdown.

The New England Patriots, led by head coach Bill Belichick and quarterback Tom Brady, entered the game with a reputation as one of the NFL's modern dynasties. This appearance marked the team's ninth trip to the Super Bowl, the most for any team at that time. For Brady and Belichick, it was an opportunity to solidify their legacy, potentially securing their fifth Super Bowl victory together. The Patriots' season had been one of strong performance, marked by Brady's exceptional play despite starting the season with a four-game suspension, a testament to the team's depth and resilience.

On the other side, the Atlanta Falcons, under head coach Dan Quinn, were seeking their first Super Bowl victory in franchise history. The Falcons had an impressive 2016 season, showcasing a high-powered offense led by quarterback Matt Ryan, who would later be named the NFL's Most Valuable Player for that season. The team's offense, also featuring standout wide receiver Julio Jones and running back Devonta Freeman, was one of the league's best, while their defense was known for its speed and aggressiveness. For the Falcons, Super Bowl LI was a chance to establish themselves as one of the NFL's elite teams and capture their first-ever championship.

The Patriots' Poor Start

The New England Patriots' performance at the start of Super Bowl LI was uncharacteristically poor, leading them to fall significantly behind the Atlanta Falcons in the first half of the game. This slow start was characterized by a series of unforced errors and unsuccessful strategies, which put them at a substantial disadvantage.

Initially, the Patriots' offense struggled to gain momentum against the Falcons' vigorous defense. Tom Brady, renowned for his precision and composure, faced immense pressure from Atlanta's pass rush. This pressure led to hurried throws and disrupted the Patriots' usually rhythmic passing game. In addition, the Falcons' defense, known for its speed and athleticism, successfully contained the Patriots' receivers, limiting their ability to make significant gains.

One of the key moments that contributed to the Patriots' poor start was Brady's interception by Falcons cornerback Robert Alford, who returned it 82 yards for a touchdown. This was a rare mistake by Brady and a pivotal play that energized the Falcons while simultaneously demoralizing the Patriots. The interception was a significant turning point in the game, as it put the Falcons ahead by a substantial margin.

Offensively, the Falcons capitalized on their opportunities, showcasing their dynamic and potent offense. Matt Ryan, executing with precision and confidence, connected with his receivers for critical gains. The Patriots' defense, despite its strategic preparations, found it challenging to contain the Falcons' versatile offensive plays.

Furthermore, New England's usually reliable special teams and defense also underperformed in the first half. They struggled to provide the offensive support typically expected in a game of this magnitude. This combination of offensive struggles, defensive lapses, and uncharacteristic errors contributed to the Patriots finding themselves in a significant deficit.

By halftime, the situation looked bleak for the Patriots. The Falcons' commanding lead was a reflection of their effective execution on both sides of the ball, while the Patriots' performance was riddled with atypical mistakes and ineffective strategies.

The Comeback

The comeback of the New England Patriots in Super Bowl LI was a remarkable display of resilience, strategic adjustments, and clutch performance. Trailing 28-3 in the third quarter, the Patriots orchestrated one of the most incredible comebacks in Super Bowl history, marked by a series of key plays and strategic shifts.

One of the critical adjustments made by the Patriots was in their offensive strategy. Recognizing the need to quickly reduce the deficit, they shifted to a more aggressive passing game. Tom Brady, displaying his legendary poise under pressure, began to find rhythm in short, quick passes that chipped away at the Falcons' defense. This change in approach helped the Patriots maintain possession and gradually build momentum.

A pivotal moment in the comeback was James White's 5-yard touchdown in the late third quarter, the first of many scores that would fuel the Patriots' resurgence. White's performance, both as a runner and a receiver, was instrumental throughout the comeback, as he provided a reliable option for Brady and consistently made crucial plays.

Another key factor in the Patriots' comeback was their defense stepping up when it mattered most. After struggling in the first half, the defense made critical stops, giving the ball back to their offense. They managed to contain the Falcons' potent offense, which had been dominant earlier in the game. Key sacks and tackles for loss helped shift the momentum towards New England.

The turning point of the game came in the fourth quarter when Brady connected with Danny Amendola for a touchdown, followed by a successful two-point conversion, bringing the score to within one possession. The tension was palpable, as the Patriots' methodical and relentless approach started to wear down the Falcons' defense.

Arguably the most iconic play of the game, and a symbol of the Patriots' comeback, was Julian Edelman's miraculous catch. With the ball tipped into the air off a defender's hands, Edelman managed to make a diving catch, just inches off the ground, amidst a tangle of players. This catch sustained a crucial drive and has since become one of the most replayed moments in Super Bowl history.

The Patriots managed to tie the game with another touchdown by White and a successful two-point conversion, completing a 25-point comeback and sending the game into overtime – a first in Super Bowl history. In overtime, the Patriots received the ball first and efficiently marched down the field, with White scoring the game-winning touchdown on a 2-yard run.

Tom Brady's Leadership

Tom Brady's leadership in the Patriots' stunning comeback during Super Bowl LI was a defining moment in his already illustrious career. His role in overturning a 28-3 deficit highlighted not just his exceptional skills as a quarterback but also his remarkable ability to inspire and galvanize his team under extreme pressure.

Throughout the game, particularly in the second half and overtime, Brady demonstrated why he is considered one of the greatest quarterbacks in NFL history. Facing a significant deficit, he maintained his composure, showcasing an unwavering confidence that seemed to invigorate his teammates. His calm demeanor in the face of adversity set the tone for the entire team, signaling that the game was far from over.

Brady's leadership was evident in his methodical dismantling of the Falcons' defense. He executed the Patriots' shift to a more aggressive passing game with precision and efficiency. His decision-making was impeccable, as he consistently found the right targets and made crucial throws under pressure. Brady's ability to read the Falcons' defense and make quick adjustments was key to the Patriots gradually chipping away at the lead.

His connection with his receivers was pivotal. Brady distributed the ball effectively, involving multiple targets and keeping the Falcons' defense off balance. His trust in his receivers, especially in critical situations, was a testament to his leadership. The iconic catch by Julian Edelman, which kept a crucial drive alive, was a product of the synergy between Brady and his receiving corps, fostered over countless practices and games.

In the huddle and on the sidelines, Brady's leadership was both vocal and by example. He rallied his teammates, encouraging them to stay focused and keep fighting. His messages were of resilience and belief, traits that he personified throughout the game. This leadership extended to moments of strategic discussion with head coach Bill Belichick and offensive coordinator Josh McDaniels, where Brady's insights and experience were invaluable in formulating the comeback strategy.

By the time the game went into overtime, Brady's leadership had already transformed the Patriots' mindset. They entered the overtime period with a palpable sense of momentum and belief, much of which stemmed from Brady's influence. In the final drive of the game, Brady's precision and control were on full display, methodically moving the team down the field before James White's game-winning touchdown.

Resilience and Never Giving Up

The remarkable comeback of the New England Patriots in Super Bowl LI was underpinned by an extraordinary display of resilience and a collective never-give-up attitude. This mindset and team spirit were pivotal in turning a seemingly impossible situation into one of the most memorable victories in NFL history.

From the outset of the second half, when the Patriots were facing a significant deficit, the team exhibited a resilience that was deeply ingrained in their ethos. This resilience was not just about physical endurance; it was also mental. The players, guided by the steady leadership of Tom Brady and the strategic acumen of head coach Bill Belichick, maintained a belief in their ability to overcome the odds. There was a palpable sense of determination, a refusal to accept defeat despite the daunting scoreboard.

This never-give-up attitude was contagious. Each successful play, each drive that culminated in points, seemed to fuel the team's belief and determination. As the Patriots started to close the gap in the score, their confidence grew, but it was a confidence tempered with focus and an understanding that there was still much work to be done. The team's ability to stay in the moment, concentrating on each play rather than the overall deficit, was crucial in maintaining their momentum.

The Patriots' resilience was also a reflection of their preparation and conditioning. The team was physically and mentally prepared for the rigors of a hard-fought game, which became evident as they outlasted the Falcons in the later stages of the match. Their conditioning, both physical and mental, allowed them to maintain a high level of play when it mattered most.

Team spirit played a significant role in the Patriots' comeback. There was a sense of unity and collective responsibility among the players. This spirit was not just about individual performances; it was about working together, supporting each other, and functioning as a cohesive unit. Each player, whether on offense, defense, or special teams, understood their role and the importance of executing it to perfection.

Furthermore, the resilience of the Patriots was rooted in their experience and history. Many of the team's players and coaches had been in high-pressure situations before, and this experience was invaluable in maintaining composure and making sound decisions under pressure. This experience, combined with a team culture that emphasized mental toughness and resilience, was evident in how the team responded to the challenge they faced.

Impact and Legacy

The impact and legacy of the New England Patriots' comeback in Super Bowl LI extend far beyond a single game or season, leaving an enduring mark on the NFL and the broader concept of perseverance in sports. This historic game not only redefined what is considered possible in a championship setting but also served as a profound illustration of resilience and determination.

In the context of the NFL, Super Bowl LI significantly elevated the narrative around comebacks and mental toughness. It challenged the conventional wisdom of what constitutes a secure lead in football, showing that no deficit is insurmountable with the right mindset and execution. This game became a benchmark for future teams, setting a new standard for what can be achieved under pressure. It also reinforced the importance of playing until the final whistle, a lesson that resonates with teams and coaches across the league.

The Patriots' comeback had a ripple effect on coaching strategies and game management in the NFL. It underscored the need for adaptability and strategic thinking throughout the entirety of a game. Coaches and players learned the importance of maintaining focus and composure, regardless of the score. The game became a case study in how to engineer a turnaround, examining the tactical adjustments made by the Patriots and how they exploited opportunities to swing the momentum in their favor.

Beyond the tactical lessons, Super Bowl LI's greatest legacy lies in its embodiment of perseverance in sports. It stands as a testament to the never-give-up attitude that is essential for success at the highest levels of competition. The game is a powerful reminder that resilience, belief, and collective effort can lead to extraordinary outcomes, even in the face of seemingly insurmountable odds.

For athletes and teams across various sports, the Patriots' comeback serves as an inspiration. It demonstrates that with determination and teamwork, remarkable feats are achievable. The game has become a motivational reference point for athletes facing adversity, encouraging them to continue striving and fighting regardless of the challenges they encounter.

The impact and legacy of Super Bowl LI resonate far beyond the New England Patriots' victory. It has left an indelible impression on the NFL, influencing coaching strategies and the approach to game management. More importantly, it has become a symbol of perseverance and resilience in sports, inspiring athletes and teams to maintain hope and determination, no matter the circumstances.

Walter Payton's Grace

Biography

Walter Payton, affectionately known as "Sweetness" for his graceful playing style and exceptional character, is a revered figure in the history of the NFL. Born on July 25, 1954, in Columbia, Mississippi, Walter Payton's journey in football began in his high school years. Despite facing initial setbacks, including being left off the high school varsity team in his sophomore year, Payton's resilience and natural talent quickly came to the forefront. By the time he was a senior, he had become a standout player, known for his speed, agility, and tenacity.

Payton's college career at Jackson State University further solidified his status as a formidable athlete. He excelled in the university's football program, amassing a series of impressive records and accolades. His time at Jackson State was marked not only by his athletic prowess but also by his academic diligence, illustrating his commitment to excellence in all facets of life.

In 1975, Walter Payton's entry into the NFL marked the beginning of what would be an extraordinary professional career. He was selected in the first round, fourth overall, by the Chicago Bears in the NFL Draft. This transition to the professional league was a significant step for Payton, who brought with him not only his athletic abilities but also a work ethic and a level of professionalism that would become his hallmarks.

From the outset of his NFL career, Payton demonstrated a unique combination of power, agility, and grace. His running style, characterized by an uncanny ability to avoid tackles and break long runs, quickly made him one of the most exciting players to watch in the league. Payton wasn't just a runner; he was also a skilled receiver and a willing blocker, making him an all-around asset to the Bears' offense.

Beyond his physical talents, Payton was known for his humility and grace. He approached the game with a respect and love that endeared him to fans and fellow players alike. His sportsmanship and dedication to the sport were evident in every game he played, making him not just a great player but also a great ambassador for football.

Career Highlights

Walter Payton's NFL career, spanning from 1975 to 1987 with the Chicago Bears, is marked by a multitude of achievements and a playing style that left an indelible mark on the sport. Known for his incredible endurance, versatility, and the poetic grace with which he played, Payton's career highlights are a testament to his status as one of the greatest running backs in NFL history.

Payton's playing style was a unique blend of agility, power, and finesse. He had an extraordinary ability to evade tackles with his elusive moves, often leaving defenders grasping at air. Payton wasn't just agile; he was also known for his remarkable strength and toughness, consistently breaking tackles and gaining extra yards through sheer willpower and effort. His endurance was legendary, as he rarely missed games and seemed to get stronger as the game progressed, embodying the workhorse running back archetype.

One of Payton's most notable career achievements was becoming the NFL's all-time leading rusher, a record he held at the time of his retirement. He amassed 16,726 rushing yards over his illustrious career, a testament to his durability and consistency. Payton also scored 110 rushing touchdowns, showcasing his effectiveness in the red zone and his role as a key player in the Bears' offense.

Payton's single-game performance on November 20, 1977, against the Minnesota Vikings was one for the ages. He rushed for an astounding 275 yards, setting an NFL record for most rushing yards in a single game, a record that stood for 23 years. This performance exemplified Payton's extraordinary talent and his ability to dominate games.

In 1977, Payton was honored as the NFL's Most Valuable Player (MVP), recognizing his contributions to the Bears and his excellence on the field. His MVP season was marked by incredible performances and leadership, further cementing his reputation as one of the league's top players.

Payton's career wasn't just about individual statistics; he was a crucial member of the 1985 Chicago Bears team that won Super Bowl XX. This victory was a crowning achievement in his career, giving him a well-deserved championship ring. Payton's contributions to the team's success were invaluable, although he was famously not given the opportunity to score a touchdown in the Super Bowl, a decision that head coach Mike Ditka later regretted.

Beyond his on-field achievements, Payton was known for his exemplary character and sportsmanship. He played the game with a level of respect and joy that endeared him to both teammates and opponents. His commitment to excellence, both on and off the field, left a lasting legacy in the NFL.

Off-field Activities and Humanitarian Work

Walter Payton's impact extended well beyond the football field, with his off-field activities and humanitarian work underscoring his commitment to making a positive difference in the lives of others. His contributions outside of football were marked by the same grace and dedication that he exhibited as a player, making him not only a legend on the field but also a respected and beloved figure in the community.

Payton's philanthropic efforts were varied and impactful. He was deeply involved in numerous charitable activities, focusing particularly on helping children and young people. One of his notable contributions was the establishment of the Walter Payton Foundation, which aimed to provide assistance and support to underprivileged children. The foundation's work included educational programs, scholarship funds, and numerous initiatives designed to uplift and empower youth.

In addition to his foundation, Payton was known for his personal involvement in charitable causes. He frequently made appearances at schools, hospitals, and community events, where he interacted with fans and community members. His visits, especially to children's hospitals, were marked by a genuine desire to bring joy and hope to those he met. Payton's warmth and kindness in these interactions left a lasting impression on those he encountered.

Payton also played a significant role in promoting organ donation. After being diagnosed with a rare liver disease in the late 1990s, he became an advocate for organ transplants and donor awareness. His openness about his condition and his efforts to raise awareness about the importance of organ donation brought national attention to the cause, potentially saving many lives.

Moreover, Payton's commitment to community and humanitarian work extended to mentoring young athletes and supporting fellow football players. He often shared his experiences and insights, helping guide the next generation of players both on and off the field. His mentorship was driven by a belief in the importance of character, discipline, and giving back, values that he consistently embodied.

Personality and Character

Payton's humility was one of his most defining traits. Despite his superstar status and numerous accolades, he remained grounded and approachable. He never sought the spotlight for personal glory but rather focused on the success of his team and the joy of playing the game. This humility endeared him to teammates, coaches, and fans alike, as he consistently deflected praise onto others and emphasized the collective effort over individual achievements.

His work ethic was legendary. Payton's commitment to excellence was evident in his rigorous training regimen and his relentless pursuit of improvement. He was known for his intense off-season workouts, which included running steep hills and extensive strength training. This dedication to conditioning not only made him one of the most durable and effective players in the NFL but also set a standard for future generations of athletes. Payton's approach to practice and preparation demonstrated his belief that talent alone was not enough; success required hard work and perseverance.

Respect for others was a cornerstone of Payton's character. He treated everyone, from teammates and coaches to fans and opponents, with kindness and consideration. His sportsmanship on the field was exemplary; he played the game with intensity but always within the bounds of fairness and respect for the competition. Off the field, Payton's interactions were marked by a genuine interest in others and a willingness to listen and engage. He valued the relationships he built throughout his life, whether in the context of football or in his broader community interactions.

Additionally, Payton's character was marked by a sense of joy and love for life. He approached both football and his off-field activities with a zest and enthusiasm that was infectious. His positive attitude, even in the face of personal and professional challenges, was a testament to his strength of character and his ability to inspire and uplift those around him.

Legacy

As a player, Payton is etched in the annals of NFL history as one of the greatest running backs ever. His record-breaking career, marked by an unmatched combination of agility, power, and endurance, set new standards for future generations of running backs. Payton's name is synonymous with greatness in football, and his playing style—characterized by its grace, tenacity, and flair—left an indelible impression on both fans and fellow players. His legacy in the sport is further immortalized by the NFL's Walter Payton Man of the Year Award, given annually to a player who exemplifies excellence on and off the field.

Beyond his athletic prowess, Payton's legacy as a person is equally significant. He is remembered for his humility, kindness, and commitment to making a positive impact in the lives of others. His philanthropic endeavors, particularly those aimed at helping children and advocating for organ donation, showcased his compassion and selflessness. Payton's approach to life, characterized by a relentless work ethic and a profound respect for others, made him a role model not just for athletes, but for people from all walks of life.

Payton's personality also left a lasting impact. His joyfulness, resilience in facing adversity, and the genuine love he had for football and life itself continue to inspire many. He approached challenges, both on and off the field, with a positive attitude and a determination to succeed, qualities that endeared him to many and contributed to his enduring legacy.

Moreover, Payton's legacy is seen in the way he influenced the culture of football and sportsmanship. He played the game with a level of integrity and honor that set a high bar for how athletes should conduct themselves in competition. His legacy continues to influence the attitudes and behaviors of players at all levels of the sport.

Life Lessons

The life of Walter Payton, marked by extraordinary grace both on and off the field, offers a wealth of lessons for individuals, providing valuable guidance on character, perseverance, and the true meaning of success.

One of the primary lessons from Payton's life is the importance of hard work and dedication. His incredible work ethic, both in training and during games, demonstrated that achieving greatness requires consistent effort and commitment.

Payton's humility, despite his immense success, is another powerful lesson. He showed that true greatness is accompanied by modesty and a willingness to share success with others. This humility, evident in the way he interacted with teammates, fans, and the community, teaches the value of remaining grounded and grateful, regardless of one's achievements.

Resilience is another key lesson from Payton's life. He faced challenges and setbacks, both on and off the field, but always demonstrated an ability to bounce back stronger. His resilience in overcoming obstacles, including injuries and defeats, exemplifies the importance of perseverance in the face of adversity.

Payton's commitment to giving back to the community and helping others is a testament to his character. His philanthropic work and advocacy for causes like organ donation highlight the importance of compassion and using one's talents and platform for the greater good.

Additionally, Payton's life teaches the value of sportsmanship and respect for the game and opponents. He played football with passion and intensity but always with a respect for the rules and the spirit of competition. This respect for the game and for others is a crucial lesson in integrity and fair play.

Lastly, Payton's joy for life and football serves as a reminder for individuals to find and pursue their passions. His love for the game was evident in every play, and his enthusiasm was contagious. This lesson underscores the importance of finding joy in one's pursuits and embracing life with a positive and passionate attitude.

Peyton Manning's Comeback

Early Career Achievements

Peyton Manning's early career in the NFL, prior to his injury, was marked by exceptional achievements and established him as one of the premier quarterbacks in the league. Born on March 24, 1976, in New Orleans, Louisiana, Peyton is the son of former NFL quarterback Archie Manning. He spent the majority of his career with the Indianapolis Colts before concluding it with the Denver Broncos. His journey from a highly touted draft pick to an NFL superstar is a testament to his skill, intelligence, and dedication to the sport.

Manning was selected as the first overall pick in the 1998 NFL Draft by the Indianapolis Colts. From the outset of his career, he showed signs of the remarkable player he would become. In his rookie season, despite facing the typical challenges of adjusting to the professional game, Manning demonstrated his potential, setting a record for most touchdown passes by a rookie.

Over the following years, Manning solidified his reputation as a top-tier quarterback. He was known for his exceptional understanding of the game, precision passing, and ability to read defenses. Manning's pre-snap adjustments and audibles became a signature aspect of his play, showcasing his football intelligence and leadership on the field.

Manning's tenure with the Colts was marked by numerous individual and team successes. He amassed a series of accolades, including multiple NFL MVP awards, and led the Colts to consistent playoff appearances. His relentless pursuit of excellence and meticulous preparation were key factors in both his individual success and the team's achievements.

One of Manning's most significant achievements with the Colts came in the 2006 season, where he led the team to victory in Super Bowl XLI against the Chicago Bears. This win not only gave Manning his first Super Bowl ring but also solidified his status as one of the great quarterbacks in NFL history.

Throughout his time with the Colts, Manning set numerous records and was consistently at the top of the league in various passing categories. He was the cornerstone of the Colts' offense, known for his ability to orchestrate high-scoring and efficient offensive drives. His leadership and performance on the field made him a beloved figure among Colts fans and respected by football enthusiasts everywhere.

Neck Injury and Recovery

Peyton Manning's career faced a significant challenge when he suffered a neck injury, leading to a complex and strenuous recovery process that tested his resilience and determination. This period marked a crucial turning point in his illustrious NFL career.

The injury, which became a major concern in 2011, was related to a bulging disc in Manning's neck. The discomfort and issues stemming from this injury were significant enough to affect his ability to play. In an effort to address the problem and return to his peak form, Manning underwent a series of neck surgeries. The most notable of these was a cervical neck fusion surgery, a procedure that involved joining selected bones in the neck.

The recovery process following the surgery was both rigorous and uncertain. Neck fusion surgery, particularly for a professional athlete like

Manning, involved a significant risk and no guarantee of returning to the previous level of performance. Manning's rehabilitation process was comprehensive, involving not just the physical aspects of recovery, but also the mental and emotional challenges that come with being away from the sport.

During his recovery, Manning faced the daunting task of retraining his body and regaining his strength. This process was arduous and required immense patience, as Manning had to slowly rebuild his neck strength and reacquaint his body with the rigors of playing professional football. His rehabilitation involved specialized exercises, physical therapy, and a gradual return to football-related activities.

The uncertainty of recovery was not just physical. Manning's future with the Indianapolis Colts, the team he had led for over a decade, became unclear. The combination of his injury, recovery, and the team's performance led to difficult decisions for both Manning and the Colts' management.

Despite these challenges, Manning's determination and work ethic during his recovery were exemplary. He remained focused on his goal of returning to the NFL, even in the face of adversity and doubt. This period of recovery not only tested his physical strength but also showcased his mental toughness and unwavering commitment to the sport he loved.

Joining the Denver Broncos

Peyton Manning's transition to the Denver Broncos marked a significant chapter in his NFL career, presenting new challenges and opportunities for the veteran quarterback. After an illustrious tenure with the Indianapolis Colts, Manning's move to Denver in 2012 was both a fresh start and a test of his ability to excel in a new environment, particularly following his recovery from neck surgery.

Manning's departure from the Colts was a momentous and emotional decision, influenced by the uncertainty surrounding his injury and the Colts' positioning for future success. As the Colts chose to rebuild with a new, younger quarterback, Manning was released, making him a free agent. This development was a turning point in his career, closing the chapter on his storied history with the Colts.

Choosing to join the Denver Broncos, Manning embarked on a journey with a team that had seen potential in him despite the risks associated with his recent injury. The Broncos, led by executive John Elway, believed in Manning's ability to lead and elevate the team, providing him with an opportunity to prove that he could still perform at an elite level.

Manning's initial challenges with the Broncos were multifaceted. Firstly, there was the physical aspect of proving that he could still play post-surgery. The football world watched with anticipation to see if Manning could regain his arm strength and durability, critical aspects of his quarterback play. There was also the challenge of adapting to a new team, system, and coaching staff, which required building chemistry with new teammates and learning new offensive schemes.

Additionally, there was the pressure of high expectations. Manning's reputation as one of the greatest quarterbacks in NFL history meant that his performance with the Broncos would be closely scrutinized. Fans and analysts were eager to see if he could replicate his success in a new setting and lead the Broncos to championship contention.

Despite these challenges, Manning approached his tenure with the Broncos with characteristic diligence and commitment. He immersed himself in learning the team's playbook, developing a rapport with his receivers, and understanding the dynamics of the Broncos' offense. His leadership and experience were immediate assets to the team, and he quickly began to make an impact on and off the field.

Winning the Super Bowl

Peyton Manning's tenure with the Denver Broncos reached a pinnacle of success with the triumphant victory in Super Bowl 50, a moment that served as the culmination of his remarkable comeback in the NFL. This achievement not only added another illustrious chapter to his career but also firmly established his legacy as one of the greatest quarterbacks in the history of the sport.

Super Bowl 50, played on February 7, 2016, saw the Broncos face off against the Carolina Panthers. Leading up to the game, there was much speculation about Manning's performance, given his age and the injuries he had overcome. However, Manning's leadership and experience proved invaluable in the high-stakes environment of the Super Bowl.

In the game, Manning demonstrated his strategic acumen, managing the offense effectively and making key plays when needed. While his statistical performance in the game was not among his most impressive, his ability to guide the team, make crucial decisions, and capitalize on the Panthers' mistakes was pivotal. His calm demeanor under pressure and his game management skills were critical components of the Broncos' strategy.

The Broncos' victory in Super Bowl 50 was a testament to the team's overall strength, particularly their formidable defense, which played a significant role in securing the win. The defense's ability to contain the Panthers' potent offense and create turnovers was key to the Broncos' success. Manning's role as a leader and a steadying influence on the team was evident throughout the game.

Manning's second Super Bowl win, and the first with the Broncos, was a significant personal triumph. It marked his return to the pinnacle of NFL success after a period of physical and professional challenges. The victory was seen by many as a validation of his resilience, skill, and determination, solidifying his status as an all-time great.

Work Ethic and Perseverance

Peyton's successful comeback after a career-threatening neck injury and subsequent transition to the Denver Broncos was underpinned by his extraordinary work ethic and perseverance. These qualities, which had been hallmarks of his career from the beginning, played a pivotal role in helping him overcome the challenges posed by his injury and return to the apex of NFL competition.

Manning's work ethic was legendary throughout his career. Known for being the first to arrive and the last to leave during practice sessions, he demonstrated an unwavering commitment to refining his skills and understanding of the game. After his neck surgery, this dedication became even more critical. Manning invested countless hours in rehabilitation, working diligently with medical professionals and trainers to regain his physical strength and conditioning. He approached his recovery with the same meticulous attention to detail that he applied to game preparation, leaving no stone unturned in his quest to return to the field.

Perseverance was another key factor in Manning's comeback. The uncertainty and physical challenges that followed his surgery would have daunted many, but Manning faced them with a steadfast resolve. He confronted setbacks during his rehabilitation process with a positive mindset, consistently focusing on his goal to return to playing at a high level. His determination during this period was a testament to his mental toughness and resilience.

Manning's ability to adapt and adjust was also crucial in overcoming his injury. He recognized the need to modify his playing style to accommodate his physical limitations post-surgery. This adaptability was evident in his play with the Broncos, where he often relied more on his mental acuity, experience, and strategic thinking than on pure physical prowess. Manning's capacity to adapt not only demonstrated his football intelligence but also his willingness to evolve as a player.

Furthermore, Manning's leadership and positive attitude were invaluable assets during his recovery. He maintained a leadership role with his team, even when he was unable to play, providing guidance and support to his teammates. His positive presence and unwavering spirit uplifted those around him and reinforced the collective resolve of the team.

Inspiration and Legacy

Peyton Manning's remarkable comeback in the NFL, culminating in a Super Bowl victory with the Denver Broncos, serves as a profound source of inspiration and cements his legacy as a symbol of resilience and dedication. His journey offers valuable lessons on the power of perseverance and the importance of commitment in the face of adversity.

Manning's comeback story teaches that resilience is a key ingredient in overcoming challenges. Facing a potentially career-ending injury and undergoing multiple surgeries, he encountered significant physical and psychological hurdles. However, his relentless determination and unwavering spirit in the face of these challenges exemplify true resilience. This aspect of his journey is particularly inspiring, demonstrating that with grit and perseverance, it's possible to surmount even the most daunting obstacles.

The dedication Manning showed during his recovery and transition to the Broncos highlights the importance of a strong work ethic and commitment to one's goals. His meticulous approach to rehabilitation, his relentless pursuit of physical and mental readiness, and his adaptation to a new team environment underscore the value of dedication in achieving success. Manning's journey is a testament to the fact that success is often a result of hard work and persistence, as much as it is of innate talent.

Manning's legacy also extends to the inspiration he provides for athletes and individuals facing their own setbacks and challenges. His story is a reminder that setbacks can be turned into comebacks with the right mindset and effort. It encourages individuals to stay focused on their goals, maintain a positive attitude, and work tirelessly towards their objectives, regardless of the obstacles they might face.

Moreover, Manning's comeback and ultimate triumph with the Broncos have solidified his status as one of the greatest quarterbacks in NFL history. His legacy is not only defined by the records he set or the games he won but also by the character he displayed throughout his career, particularly during its most challenging phase. He is remembered not just as a great athlete but as an individual who embodied the principles of resilience, dedication, and sportsmanship.

The Immaculate Reception

The 1972 Playoff Game

The 1972 AFC Divisional Playoff game, which set the stage for the iconic moment known as the "Immaculate Reception," is etched in NFL history as one of the most dramatic and memorable games. Held on December 23, 1972, the game featured the Pittsburgh Steelers and the Oakland Raiders, two powerhouse teams of the era, clashing in a fiercely competitive battle.

The game took place at Three Rivers Stadium in Pittsburgh, Pennsylvania. The atmosphere was electric, with a palpable sense of anticipation among the fans. Pittsburgh, known for its passionate and loyal fan base, was buzzing with excitement, as the Steelers had made it to the playoffs for the first time in 25 years. The Raiders, on the other hand, were an established force in the league, having been playoff contenders consistently in the preceding years.

The game itself was a defensive struggle, characterized by hard hits and a tactical battle between two well-matched teams. Both the Steelers and the Raiders showcased their defensive prowess, making it difficult for either offense to gain significant ground. The scoring was minimal, reflecting the intensity and toughness of the play.

As the game progressed, the tension mounted, with each team understanding the high stakes of a playoff victory. The Steelers, led by coach Chuck Noll, were looking to make a statement in their first playoff appearance in decades. The Raiders, under the leadership of coach John Madden, were determined to continue their legacy of success.

Heading into the final moments of the game, the Steelers were trailing the Raiders by a single point, with the score at 7-6. The situation seemed dire for Pittsburgh, as they faced a fourth down with only 22 seconds left on the clock. The Steelers' hopes of advancing in the playoffs were hanging by a thread, setting the scene for one of the most extraordinary and debated plays in NFL history.

The Play

The scene was set with the Pittsburgh Steelers in a desperate situation, facing a fourth-and-10 on their own 40-yard line, with only 22 seconds remaining in the game and trailing the Oakland Raiders 7-6. Steelers quarterback Terry Bradshaw took the snap and dropped back to pass under heavy pressure from the Raiders' defense. As the Raiders' defenders closed in, Bradshaw unleashed a desperate throw downfield towards running back John "Frenchy" Fuqua.

As the ball approached Fuqua, he collided with Raiders safety Jack Tatum, known for his hard-hitting style. The ball ricocheted off one of the players - it remains a subject of debate whether it hit Fuqua, Tatum, or both - and took an improbable bounce back towards the line of scrimmage.

In a stroke of extraordinary luck and timing, Steelers rookie running back Franco Harris, who had initially been blocking on the play, reacted swiftly to the deflected ball. Harris scooped up the ball just inches from the turf and took off down the sideline. With Raiders players in pursuit, Harris sprinted 42 yards to the end zone, scoring the game-winning touchdown as time expired.

The play immediately sparked a frenzy in Three Rivers Stadium. Steelers fans erupted in jubilation, hardly believing the miraculous turn of events. On the field, players and coaches were equally astonished. The Steelers celebrated the incredible play, while the Raiders stood in disbelief, some protesting that the play had been illegal. Under the NFL rules at the time, a pass could not be legally caught by an offensive player if it first bounced off another offensive player, but could if it bounced off a defensive player.

The officials conferred for several minutes, adding to the tension and drama. Finally, they ruled the play a touchdown, cementing the Steelers' 13-7 victory and sending them to the AFC Championship Game.

The "Immaculate Reception" has since become a legendary moment in NFL lore. It is celebrated by Steelers fans as a miraculous and pivotal play in the franchise's history, while for Raiders fans, it remains a controversial and painful memory. The play's name, coined by Steelers fans and the media, reflects its almost miraculous nature, and it continues to be a subject of fascination and debate among football enthusiasts.

Controversy and Analysis

The central controversy revolved around the then-existing NFL rule, which stated that a pass could not be legally caught by an offensive player if it first bounced off another offensive player. The ambiguity arose from whether the ball, thrown by Terry Bradshaw, first made contact with Steelers' running back Frenchy Fuqua or Raiders' safety Jack Tatum, or both. If the ball had only hit Fuqua, the play would have been illegal. However, if it had touched Tatum or both players, Harris' catch would be legal.

No conclusive video evidence exists to clarify this point definitively, as the available footage did not provide a clear angle on the crucial moment of the play. This lack of definitive evidence has led to ongoing debates among fans, players, and analysts. Raiders fans and players, in particular, have often contended that the play should have been ruled illegal, believing that the ball only contacted Fuqua.

The play has been dissected and analyzed from multiple angles, with various experts and enthusiasts offering their interpretations. Technological advancements have allowed for enhanced reviews of the play, but even with these tools, a definitive conclusion remains elusive. The play's mystery is compounded by the participants' accounts, as both Fuqua and Tatum provided ambiguous or conflicting statements over the years.

The controversy surrounding the "Immaculate Reception" also highlights the evolution of NFL rules and officiating. The play was a catalyst for discussions about instant replay and the need for clearer rules regarding possession and deflections. In many ways, the play's ambiguous nature exposed the limitations of officiating at the time and the need for technological aid in making accurate calls.

Furthermore, the "Immaculate Reception" has a symbolic significance beyond the controversy. For Steelers fans, it's a symbol of a miraculous turn of fortune, marking the beginning of a successful era in the franchise's history. For Raiders fans, it's often viewed as a symbol of injustice and a turning point in a rivalry marked by intense competition.

Impact on the Steelers and NFL

For the Pittsburgh Steelers, the play marked a turning point in their history. Prior to this moment, the Steelers had experienced limited success, with few playoff appearances and no championship victories. The "Immaculate Reception" seemed to catalyze a change in fortune for the team. It occurred during a critical playoff game and led to the Steelers' victory, propelling them into the AFC Championship Game. This play is often seen as the beginning of a golden era for the Steelers, who would go on to become one of the most successful franchises in the NFL in the 1970s.

The play's impact extended beyond that single season, contributing to the development of a winning culture within the Steelers organization. It helped build confidence and a sense of destiny, elements that played a decisive role in the team's subsequent successes, including four Super Bowl victories in the next six years. The "Immaculate Reception" symbolized a shift in the Steelers' identity from perennial underdogs to dominant contenders.

In the broader context of the NFL, the play holds a special place in the league's history due to its dramatic and improbable nature. It is frequently featured in discussions about the greatest and most memorable moments in football, capturing the imagination of fans and players alike. The play's significance is reflected in its enduring presence in NFL lore, where it continues to be a subject of fascination and debate.

The "Immaculate Reception" also had implications for the NFL in terms of rules and officiating. The controversy surrounding the play highlighted the need for clearer rules and eventually contributed to the development and refinement of instant replay technology. This shift towards using technology to aid in officiating decisions can be traced back, in part, to the ambiguity and debate sparked by this iconic play.

Additionally, the play has become a cultural touchstone, transcending the sport itself. It is referenced in various forms of media and is part of the collective memory of American football. The "Immaculate Reception" serves as a reminder of the unpredictability of sports and the extraordinary moments that can arise in the heat of competition.

Symbol of Hope and Luck

The play is often viewed as a symbol of luck or serendipity. The way the ball ricocheted off the players and landed perfectly for Franco Harris making the catch was a once-in-a-lifetime occurrence, illustrating how elements of chance can significantly influence defining outcomes. For many, the "Immaculate Reception" encapsulates the idea that, sometimes, success involves an element of luck, beyond skill and preparation.

However, the play also epitomizes the importance of readiness and the ability to seize opportunities. While luck played a part in how the events unfolded, it was Harris' alertness and quick reaction that ultimately made the difference. His ability to capitalize on the unexpected chance illustrates the significance of being prepared to act when opportunities arise. Harris' response to the play serves as a lesson in staying focused, being adaptable, and making the most of unforeseen circumstances.

For the Steelers and their fans, the "Immaculate Reception" has become a symbol of hope. It represents the idea that no matter how dire the situation may seem, there is always the possibility of a positive turn of events. This message of hope has resonated with the Steelers' fan base and has become a part of the team's identity.

Moreover, the play is often invoked as a metaphor for resilience and perseverance. It signifies that even in moments of uncertainty or when the odds seem insurmountable, determination and readiness can lead to remarkable achievements. This aspect of the play is particularly inspiring, offering a message of encouragement to persist in the face of challenges.

In the broader context of sports and beyond, the "Immaculate Reception" serves as a reminder of the unpredictable nature of life and the potential for extraordinary moments to occur. It encourages both athletes and individuals to remain vigilant for opportunities and underscores the notion that luck, when combined with preparedness and action, can lead to incredible outcomes.

Legacy in Sports Lore

In the realm of football folklore, the "Immaculate Reception" is celebrated as one of the most miraculous and unforgettable plays ever. It has become a staple of NFL history, often featured in highlight reels, documentaries, and discussions about the greatest moments in the sport. The play's dramatic nature, the high stakes involved, and the controversy surrounding it have contributed to its enduring appeal and intrigue.

The legacy of the "Immaculate Reception" is also evident in its influence on the culture of football. It has become a symbol of the unexpected and exhilarating nature of the sport, where a single play can change the course of a game, a season, or even a franchise's history. The play is a reminder of why fans love football - for its capacity to produce moments of sheer wonder and disbelief.

Moreover, the play has a special significance for the Pittsburgh Steelers and their fans. It is seen as a pivotal turning point in the franchise's history, marking the beginning of a period of dominance in the NFL. The "Immaculate Reception" is woven into the fabric of the Steelers' identity and is a source of pride and tradition for the team and its supporters.

The play's legacy extends to the players involved, particularly Franco Harris, who made the miraculous catch. Harris' career and legacy are inextricably linked to this moment, which showcased his athleticism and instinctive play. The "Immaculate Reception" has become a defining highlight of his career, remembered and celebrated by football fans around the world.

In addition, the "Immaculate Reception" continues to be a subject of fascination and debate among football enthusiasts. The play's controversial nature has sparked endless discussions and analyses, adding to its mythic status. It serves as a conversation starter and a point of connection for fans, fostering a sense of community and shared history.

Sarah Fuller's Historic Kick

Background

Sarah Fuller's historic journey to a groundbreaking moment in football began with her career in another sport: soccer. Fuller's background as a soccer player laid the foundation for her eventual transition into football history, showcasing her athletic skills and pioneering spirit.

Born on June 20, 1999, in Wylie, Texas, Fuller grew up with a passion for soccer, dedicating herself to the sport from a young age. Her talent and hard work in soccer led her to play at the collegiate level, where she became a key player for the Vanderbilt University women's soccer team. As a goalkeeper for Vanderbilt, Fuller demonstrated remarkable skills, including agility, strong decision-making, and leadership on the field. These qualities were pivotal in her soccer career and would later become instrumental in her historic transition to football.

During her time with the Vanderbilt soccer team, Fuller was known for her competitiveness and work ethic. She played an integral role in the team's defense, consistently delivering performances that helped secure victories and uphold the team's competitive standing. Her ability to perform under pressure and maintain composure in high-stakes situations was a testament to her athletic prowess and mental toughness.

Fuller's success in soccer was marked by team achievements and personal accolades, reflecting her impact as a player. She was part of a Vanderbilt team that made significant strides in collegiate soccer, contributing to its defensive strength. Her leadership qualities were also recognized by her teammates and coaches, as she often stepped up in crucial moments to guide and motivate the team.

Transition to Football

In the fall of 2020, the Vanderbilt football team found itself in a challenging situation due to the COVID-19 pandemic. Several of the team's specialists, including kickers, were unavailable for a game against the Missouri Tigers due to COVID-19 protocols. This situation led the football team's coaching staff to look for alternatives within the university's athletic programs.

Aware of Fuller's accomplishments as a goalkeeper for the Vanderbilt women's soccer team, the football coaches recognized potential in her strong kicking ability. They approached Fuller with the opportunity to join the football team as a kicker. Fuller, fresh off her participation in the SEC Championship with the soccer team, accepted the offer, seeing it as a chance to contribute to another Vanderbilt sports team and embrace a new athletic challenge.

Fuller's decision to join the football team was a significant one, not just for her but for the sport of football. By agreeing to play as a kicker, she was set to break barriers in an overwhelmingly male-dominated sport. Her willingness to step into this new role demonstrated her courage and commitment to pushing boundaries in collegiate sports.

Fuller's transition to football involved a rapid adjustment period. She had to acclimate to the different techniques and dynamics of football kicking, as opposed to soccer goalkeeping. Her practice sessions with the football team were focused on honing her skills for kickoffs and point-after attempts, translating her soccer skills into football proficiency.

The Historic Game

Sarah Fuller's historic moment in football occurred on November 28, 2020, during a game that would etch her name in the annals of sports history. This game, where she took to the field as a kicker for the Vanderbilt University football team, marked a groundbreaking moment in the traditionally male-dominated sport of college football.

The game was an SEC matchup between Vanderbilt and the University of Missouri. Held at Memorial Stadium in Columbia, Missouri, the game drew significant attention, not just for the competition itself, but for the anticipation of Fuller's participation. Her presence on the roster had made national headlines, sparking conversations about gender barriers in sports.

Fuller's opportunity came on November 28, after halftime. Vanderbilt, trailing in the game, turned to Fuller to execute the second-half kickoff. This moment was laden with significance, as it marked the first time a woman played in a Power Five conference football game, the highest level of college football in the United States.

Dressed in Vanderbilt gear with the words "Play Like a Girl" on the back of her helmet, a nod to the slogan promoting female participation in sports, Fuller approached the kickoff with confidence. She executed a perfectly-placed squib kick that was downed by Missouri at their 35-yard line, ensuring no return. While the kick was tactically planned, it was also symbolic, representing a barrier-breaking moment in the sport.

Fuller's historic play was met with widespread recognition and celebration. Her teammates and coaches, along with the spectators, acknowledged the significance of the moment. The impact of her participation transcended the game's score or outcome, marking a milestone for gender inclusion and diversity in sports.

Her participation in this game was not only a personal achievement for Fuller but also a monumental step forward for women in sports. It challenged long-standing gender norms and inspired countless young girls and women, demonstrating that opportunities in sports should not be limited by gender.

Challenges and Reaction

One of the primary challenges Fuller faced was the physical and technical transition from soccer to football. Kicking a football, especially in a game situation, required adapting her soccer skills to the nuances of football, a challenge she embraced with determination. Additionally, the intense scrutiny and pressure that came with being in the national spotlight presented a mental and emotional challenge. Fuller had to navigate this while staying focused on her performance.

There was also the challenge of entering a male-dominated sport, where female participation at this level was unprecedented. Fuller had to integrate into the team and adapt to a new sporting environment, all under the watchful eyes of the media and the public. This situation required not only physical skill and mental toughness but also a strong sense of self-confidence and resilience.

The public reaction to Fuller's participation was mixed, though largely positive and supportive. Many people, including prominent figures in sports and other fields, praised her for breaking barriers and setting an example for young girls and women. Her appearance was seen as a significant step forward for gender equality in sports, inspiring countless aspiring female athletes.

However, Fuller's role as a trailblazer also attracted criticism and skepticism from some quarters. Critics questioned the quality of her play and the motives behind her inclusion on the team. This criticism was part of the broader discourse about the place of women in traditionally male-dominated sports.

Fuller's teammates and the Vanderbilt community largely supported her. They recognized the courage and commitment it took for her to step into this new role and appreciated the attention and conversation her participation brought to the team and the university.

Additionally, Fuller's achievement sparked discussions in the wider sports community about opportunities for women in sports, challenging traditional gender norms and highlighting the need for greater inclusivity. Her historic kick was not just a personal achievement but a moment that prompted reflection on the progress and potential in women's sports.

Gender Barriers in Sports

Fuller's accomplishment is particularly noteworthy considering the landscape of college football, a sport that has traditionally been an exclusively male domain, especially at the Power Five conference level. Her presence on the field challenged the preconceived notions about the roles and capabilities of female athletes in such a high-profile and physically demanding sport. It sent a powerful message that skill and talent are not confined by gender.

The significance of Fuller's achievement extends beyond her personal accomplishment; it symbolizes the broader struggle for gender equality in sports. Her participation in a college football game highlighted the disparities that still exist in athletic opportunities and recognition between men and women. It brought to light the ongoing need to advocate for equal opportunities for female athletes in all sports, including those traditionally dominated by men.

Fuller's role in breaking gender barriers also served as an inspiration for young girls and women with aspirations in sports, demonstrating that the boundaries of what is possible are continually expanding. Her story is a vivid example that can encourage young female athletes to pursue their sporting ambitions, even in fields where they may be underrepresented.

Furthermore, her achievement prompted discussions about how sports organizations, from youth leagues to professional levels, can create more inclusive environments. It underscored the importance of providing support systems, resources, and equitable opportunities for female athletes. Fuller's participation in a football game is a reminder of the need for ongoing advocacy and action to ensure that gender does not limit access to sports and athletic development.

In the larger societal context, Fuller's historic kick resonates beyond the realm of sports, contributing to the dialogue about gender roles and equality in various sectors. It illustrates how sports can be a catalyst for social change and a platform for challenging stereotypes and advocating for equality.

Role Model and Inspiration

Sarah Fuller's story transcends the realm of sports, positioning her as a role model and source of inspiration for young girls and boys alike. Her groundbreaking achievement in college football exemplifies qualities such as courage, perseverance, and the willingness to challenge norms, making her an influential figure for the younger generation.

For young girls, Fuller's journey is a powerful illustration of breaking gender barriers and challenging societal expectations. Her success in a male-dominated sport provides tangible proof that girls can aspire to and achieve greatness in any field they choose, regardless of traditional gender roles. Fuller's story sends a message of empowerment, encouraging young girls to pursue their passions and dreams with confidence, even in areas where they may be underrepresented.

Boys, too, can draw inspiration from Fuller's story. It teaches them the importance of inclusivity and respect for diversity in all aspects of life, including sports. Seeing a woman excel in a role traditionally held by men can help young boys understand and appreciate the value of equality and the need to support and celebrate achievements irrespective of gender. Fuller's story can contribute to shaping a more equitable mindset in boys from a young age.

Moreover, Fuller's embodiment of resilience and determination in the face of challenges is a universal lesson. Her ability to step into a high-pressure situation, adapt to a new environment, and perform with composure is inspirational for all young people. It underscores the virtues of hard work, dedication, and staying focused on one's goals, regardless of the obstacles.

Fuller also represents the importance of seizing opportunities and being open to new experiences. Her willingness to take on a challenge outside her comfort zone is a valuable lesson in personal growth and exploration. This aspect of her story encourages young people to be open-minded and courageous in exploring their own potential and interests.

In addition to her achievements on the field, Fuller's positive attitude, team spirit, and advocacy for inclusivity make her a role model off the field. Her engagement with initiatives like "Play Like a Girl" and her advocacy for female participation in sports serve as further inspiration, highlighting her commitment to making a difference beyond her athletic accomplishments.

Sarah Fuller's role as a model and inspiration is significant for young girls and boys. Her story is a compelling example of challenging gender norms, demonstrating resilience, and embracing opportunities. It inspires young people to pursue their dreams with determination and confidence, promotes inclusivity and equality, and highlights the importance of hard work and a positive attitude in achieving one's goals.

The Ice Bowl

Setting the Stage

The 1967 NFL Championship game, famously known as the "Ice Bowl," is one of the most legendary games in the history of the league, remembered particularly for its brutal weather conditions and the high stakes involved. Played on December 31, 1967, the game set the stage for a dramatic and enduring chapter in NFL lore.

The game was a showdown between the Green Bay Packers and the Dallas Cowboys, held at Lambeau Field in Green Bay, Wisconsin. The stakes were incredibly high, as the game would determine the National Football League champion for the 1967 season and decide who would go on to play in Super Bowl II.

However, what made the Ice Bowl particularly infamous were the extreme weather conditions. On game day, Green Bay was gripped by a brutal cold wave. Temperatures plummeted to a bone-chilling -13 degrees Fahrenheit (-25 degrees Celsius), with the wind chill pushing it down to a staggering -48 degrees Fahrenheit (-44 degrees Celsius). These were some of the coldest conditions ever recorded for an NFL game, earning the matchup its nickname.

The frigid temperatures had a significant impact on the game. The field itself, despite having an underground heating system, froze into a hard, icy surface, earning it the moniker of "the frozen tundra." Players struggled with the cold, dealing with issues like frostbite and difficulty breathing. The icy field conditions also affected the game's play, as it was challenging for players to get traction and maintain their footing.

The atmosphere in the stadium was electric, despite the bitter cold. Fans braved the extreme temperatures to support their teams, bundled up in layers of clothing. The Packers, led by the legendary coach Vince Lombardi, were seeking their third consecutive NFL championship, adding to the game's intensity. The Cowboys, under coach Tom Landry, were aiming to dethrone the Packers and claim their first NFL title.

Gameplay in Extreme Conditions

The gameplay of the 1967 NFL Championship, known as the Ice Bowl, was profoundly affected by the extreme cold conditions, presenting unique challenges for both the Green Bay Packers and the Dallas Cowboys. The frigid temperatures and icy field significantly influenced the strategies, performance, and physical well-being of the players.

In these severe conditions, the physical toll on the players was evident. The brutal cold made it difficult for them to stay warm and maintain flexibility, affecting their speed, agility, and overall performance. Players faced the risk of frostbite, and the cold air made breathing painful, adding to the physical strain of the game. Despite wearing thermal clothing, heated benches, and other measures to combat the cold, the players were visibly affected by the extreme weather.

The icy surface of Lambeau Field, notoriously hard and slippery due to the sub-zero temperatures, altered the dynamics of the game. Players struggled for traction, leading to more slipping and falling than in typical games. This affected everything from the effectiveness of running plays to the ability of receivers and defenders to make sharp cuts. The passing game was also impacted, as quarterbacks found it challenging to grip and throw the ball accurately in the freezing conditions.

The extreme weather necessitated adjustments in game strategies. Both teams had to rely more on short, strategic plays rather than long passes or complex formations that required precise movements. The running game became more critical, though ball carriers faced their challenges with the slippery ball and icy turf.

Defensively, players had to adjust their techniques to ensure stability and balance, as the usual quick movements and hard tackles were riskier on the frozen field. The game became as much about managing the conditions as it was about outmaneuvering the opponent.

Coaches Vince Lombardi of the Packers and Tom Landry of the Cowboys faced the challenge of adapting their game plans to the conditions. Their decisions on play-calling and player rotations were crucial in a game where endurance and resilience were as important as skill and strategy.

Key Moments and Players

One of the most pivotal figures in the game was Bart Starr, the quarterback for the Green Bay Packers. Starr's leadership and poise under pressure were critical to the Packers' offense. Despite the difficult conditions, he managed to execute plays with precision and calmness. His ability to adapt to the icy field and maintain control of the game was a testament to his skill and experience.

The game's defining moment came in its final seconds. With just 16 seconds left on the clock and the Packers trailing by three points, Starr executed one of the most famous plays in NFL history. In a gutsy call, Starr ran a quarterback sneak on the 1-yard line, successfully crossing into the end zone for the game-winning touchdown. This play, known as "the sneak," is forever etched in the annals of the NFL as a symbol of grit and determination.

Another key player in the game was Packers' running back Donny Anderson. In the treacherous conditions, Anderson's efforts were crucial in gaining hard-earned yards on the ground. His ability to navigate the icy turf and maintain possession under challenging conditions was vital for the Packers' offense.

On the defensive side, the Packers' Ray Nitschke played a significant role. His performance in the linebacker position was critical in halting the Cowboys' offense. Nitschke's leadership on the field helped galvanize the Packers' defense against the formidable Dallas team.

For the Dallas Cowboys, quarterback Don Meredith was a standout player. Meredith faced immense pressure from the Packers' defense but managed to lead his team with composure. His throws and strategic play-calling kept the Cowboys competitive throughout the game.

Wide receiver Lance Rentzel of the Cowboys also made significant contributions. Rentzel's receptions were crucial in advancing the Cowboys' offense, and his ability to make catches in the harsh conditions demonstrated his skill and adaptability.

The Ice Bowl was not just a display of individual talent but also a testament to team effort and strategic coaching. Vince Lombardi and Tom Landry, coaches for the Packers and Cowboys respectively, demonstrated their strategic prowess, making critical decisions that influenced the course of the game.

Mental and Physical Toughness

The Ice Bowl, played under some of the harshest conditions in NFL history, was a profound testament to the mental and physical toughness displayed by the players of both the Green Bay Packers and the Dallas Cowboys. The extreme cold and challenging field conditions required an extraordinary level of endurance and resilience from every player on the field.

Physically, the players were pushed to their limits. The sub-zero temperatures posed a significant challenge, affecting muscle function, agility, and overall physical performance. Players had to combat the risk of frostbite and hypothermia while engaging in intense physical activity. The ability to maintain focus on the game, execute plays, and withstand hits in such conditions demonstrated remarkable physical fortitude.

The icy field added another layer to the physical challenge. Players had to adjust their movements and tactics to avoid slips and falls, which required not only physical skill but also a heightened awareness of the playing surface. The effort to stay upright and effective in such an environment, while battling the extreme cold, spoke volumes about their physical toughness and adaptability.

Mentally, the players exhibited exceptional toughness and focus. Playing in such extreme weather conditions required a strong mental attitude. The ability to concentrate on the game, execute strategic plays, and maintain a competitive edge under such circumstances was a significant mental challenge. Players had to mentally overcome the discomfort and distractions posed by the cold, channeling their focus solely on the game.

The endurance shown by the players was also remarkable. As the game progressed, fatigue set in, exacerbated by the cold. The players' ability to continue performing at a high level, pushing through fatigue and the physical discomforts of the cold, was a testament to their stamina and endurance.

Moreover, the game required a high level of mental resilience. The pressure of a championship game, combined with the adverse weather conditions, could easily have overwhelmed the players. Yet, they demonstrated remarkable composure and mental strength, particularly in the game's critical moments, such as Bart Starr's game-winning quarterback sneak in the final seconds.

Outcome and Aftermath

The outcome of the Ice Bowl had significant and lasting implications for both the Green Bay Packers and the Dallas Cowboys, as well as for the players involved. The game, which ended with a narrow 21-17 victory for the Packers, had a profound impact on the legacy of both teams and the individuals who played in it.

For the Green Bay Packers, the victory in the Ice Bowl solidified their status as one of the NFL's most dominant teams of the era. It marked their third consecutive NFL Championship, a remarkable feat that underscored the team's prowess and the effective leadership of coach Vince Lombardi. The win also secured the Packers' place in Super Bowl II, where they would go on to achieve another victory, further cementing their legacy in the annals of football history.

The game's outcome was a pivotal moment for several Packers players. Quarterback Bart Starr, whose game-winning quarterback sneak became an iconic moment in NFL history, enhanced his reputation as a clutch performer and one of the greatest quarterbacks of his time. The resilience and toughness demonstrated by the Packers' players in the Ice Bowl added to their individual legacies and the team's lore.

For the Dallas Cowboys, the loss was a bitter pill to swallow. Coming so close to victory only to fall short in the final moments was a devastating outcome. However, the game also served as a catalyst for the Cowboys, who would go on to become a dominant force in the NFL in the ensuing years. The experience of the Ice Bowl, while painful, contributed to the team's growth and eventual success, including multiple Super Bowl victories in the 1970s.

The Ice Bowl also had a profound personal impact on the players. The physical and mental demands of the game, played in such extreme conditions, were a true test of endurance and resilience. For many players, the Ice Bowl remained one of the most memorable and defining moments of their careers. The game's legacy continued to be a point of reflection for the players, as they recalled the challenges and triumphs of that historic day.

In the broader context of the NFL, the Ice Bowl became a symbol of the harsh and unpredictable nature of football, as well as the incredible perseverance and determination required to succeed in the sport. The game's dramatic finish and the extreme weather conditions in which it was played have ensured its place in NFL folklore, often referenced in discussions about the greatest games in football history.

Lessons in Resilience

The Ice Bowl, with its extreme weather conditions and high-stakes gameplay, offers valuable lessons in resilience, teaching how to cope with and overcome adverse situations. This legendary game serves as a powerful metaphor for the challenges faced in sports and life, highlighting the virtues of perseverance, adaptability, and mental fortitude.

One key lesson from the Ice Bowl is the importance of preparation and adaptability in the face of adversity. The players and coaches had to adjust their strategies and techniques to contend with the extreme cold and icy field. This adaptability is a vital skill, not just in sports, but in any challenging situation. It teaches that while one cannot always control the circumstances, the ability to adapt and find ways to succeed within those constraints is essential.

The game also exemplifies the importance of mental toughness. The players had to maintain focus and composure despite the physical discomfort and the high-pressure environment. This mental resilience is critical in overcoming difficult situations. It shows the power of a positive mindset and determination in facing challenges, whether on the football field, in personal endeavors, or in professional pursuits.

Another lesson from the Ice Bowl is the significance of teamwork and collective effort in overcoming adversity. The challenging conditions of the game required players to rely on each other and work together cohesively. This sense of teamwork underscores the value of collaboration and support in difficult times. It demonstrates that often, the best way to overcome adversity is by leaning on and working with others.

The players' endurance and persistence in the Ice Bowl are also instructive. The ability to keep pushing forward, even when conditions are harsh and the odds seem insurmountable, is a testament to the human spirit. This endurance is a powerful lesson in not giving up, showing that persistence and hard work can lead to success, even in the most daunting circumstances.

Finally, the Ice Bowl teaches the value of perspective in facing challenges. For the players and fans, the game was more than just a contest; it was a test of character and a memorable experience that lasted a lifetime. This perspective helps in understanding that sometimes, the journey and the lessons learned in facing adversity can be as valuable as the outcome itself.

Derrick Coleman's Inspiring Journey

Early Life and Challenges

Derrick Coleman's inspiring journey to the NFL is marked by his remarkable resilience and determination in the face of significant challenges. Born on October 18, 1990, in West Los Angeles, California, Coleman faced a major life challenge from a young age: he was diagnosed with a genetic hearing impairment when he was just three years old. This condition left him legally deaf, presenting a unique set of challenges that he would navigate throughout his life and athletic career.

Growing up, Coleman wore hearing aids and learned to read lips to communicate effectively. His hearing impairment posed various obstacles, particularly in social and educational settings, where he often had to contend with misunderstandings and a lack of awareness about his condition. Despite these challenges, Coleman showed an early resilience and a determination not to let his hearing impairment define him or limit his potential.

His journey into football began in his school years, where his talent and passion for the sport became evident. Coleman faced additional challenges on the football field due to his hearing impairment. The noisy environment of football games and practices made communication difficult, as it was hard to hear calls and signals. However, he adapted by using his hearing aids and relying on his ability to read lips and pay close attention to visual cues.

Coleman's early life was not just about overcoming the challenges of being deaf; it was also about proving his abilities and worth both on and off the field. He worked tirelessly to improve his football skills, showing a natural aptitude for the sport. His dedication and hard work were evident, as he excelled in high school football, becoming a standout player.

His determination to succeed despite his hearing impairment was a source of inspiration to those around him. Coleman didn't view his deafness as a disability, but rather as a challenge to be overcome. This mindset would be a guiding principle throughout his life, driving him to break barriers and achieve his dreams against the odds.

Path to the NFL

After a successful high school football career, Coleman attended the University of California, Los Angeles (UCLA), where he played as a fullback for the Bruins. At UCLA, he demonstrated his formidable skills on the field, combining power and agility to become a key player in the team's offense. Coleman's time in college was not just about showcasing his athletic abilities; it also involved honing his skills to communicate effectively on the field despite his hearing impairment.

Coleman's performance at UCLA set the stage for his entry into professional football. However, his path to the NFL was not straightforward. In the 2012 NFL Draft, Coleman went undrafted, a setback that would have deterred many but only fueled his determination. His response to this disappointment was to work even harder, remaining steadfast in his goal to play in the NFL.

Coleman's perseverance paid off when he signed as an undrafted free agent with the Minnesota Vikings. Although his time with the Vikings was short-lived, he did not give up on his dream. He continued to train and improve, showcasing the tenacity that had characterized his journey so far.

His breakthrough came when he signed with the Seattle Seahawks. With the Seahawks, Coleman's career took a significant turn. He became an integral part of the team, contributing both on special teams and as a fullback. His ability to read the game, combined with his physical prowess, made him a valuable asset to the team.

Coleman's presence in the NFL was groundbreaking. As the first legally deaf offensive player in the NFL, he broke significant barriers and served as an inspiration to many. His journey to the NFL highlighted not just his exceptional talent as a football player but also the importance of resilience, adaptability, and sheer determination in overcoming challenges.

Overcoming Communication Barriers

Derrick Coleman's journey in the NFL was not only remarkable for his athletic prowess but also for how he adeptly overcame communication barriers related to his deafness. His ability to adapt to these challenges in the professional football environment is a significant aspect of his inspiring story.

In the fast-paced and often noisy world of NFL games, effective communication is fundamental. For Coleman, who is legally deaf, this presented a unique set of challenges. He tackled these obstacles head-on, using a combination of technology, visual cues, and personal strategies to ensure effective communication on and off the field.

One of the key adaptations Coleman made was the use of specially designed hearing aids. These devices were tailored to withstand the rigors of a football game, including the physical contact and the sweat and moisture of intense physical exertion. The hearing aids helped amplify sounds, allowing Coleman to hear calls and signals better.

In addition to technological aids, Coleman heavily relied on lip-reading to understand his teammates and coaches. This skill, which he had honed since childhood, was invaluable in helping him pick up instructions and cues during games and practices. His ability to read lips was complemented by his teammates and coaches, who were mindful of facing him when speaking to ensure clear communication.

Coleman also utilized visual signals on the field. He paid close attention to the physical cues and hand signals from his teammates and coaches. This visual communication was crucial during loud games where hearing aids were less effective due to the overwhelming noise in the stadium.

Another important aspect of Coleman's communication strategy was his proactive approach. He made it a point to familiarize himself thoroughly with the playbook and game plans. This preparation meant he often knew what to expect on the field, reducing the need for on-the-spot verbal communication.

The Seattle Seahawks, in turn, showed commendable inclusivity in accommodating Coleman's needs. The team and staff embraced the challenge of effective communication, demonstrating an awareness and sensitivity to Coleman's situation. This collaborative effort was a testament to the team's cohesion and adaptability.

Success with the Seahawks

During his stint with the Seahawks, Coleman established himself as a reliable and versatile player. He excelled in the role of a fullback and was a key contributor on special teams. His physicality, combined with his keen understanding of the game, made him an asset in blocking schemes and in executing plays that required precision and force. Coleman's ability to perform various roles showcased his adaptability and commitment to the team's success.

Coleman's contributions were not limited to his on-field performance. He was also an integral part of the team's locker room dynamics, bringing an inspiring presence and a positive attitude. His journey to the NFL and his ability to overcome challenges resonated with his teammates, making him a motivational figure within the Seahawks organization.

His most significant contribution came during the Seahawks' successful 2013 season, which culminated in their victory in Super Bowl XLVIII. Coleman's role in this championship run was decisive. He contributed significantly on special teams and as a fullback, helping to bolster the Seahawks' powerful offense and effective special teams unit. His performance in the Super Bowl and throughout the season was a reflection of his hard work and dedication to his craft.

In Super Bowl XLVIII, held on February 2, 2014, against the Denver Broncos, Coleman's contributions, though not headline-grabbing, were vital to the team's dominant performance. The Seahawks' victory in the Super Bowl was a team effort, and Coleman's role was a testament to the importance of every player's contribution, regardless of the prominence of their role.

Off the field, Coleman's presence in the Super Bowl also carried significant symbolic weight. As the first legally deaf offensive player to participate in a Super Bowl, he broke barriers and set an inspiring example. His participation in the Super Bowl was a moment of pride not just for him but also for the deaf and hard-of-hearing community, showcasing the possibilities for athletes with disabilities at the highest levels of sports.

Advocacy and Impact

Coleman has used his platform as a professional athlete to shed light on the challenges faced by the deaf and hard-of-hearing community. He has been vocal about his own experiences, sharing his story to inspire and empower others who face similar challenges. By openly discussing the obstacles he overcame, Coleman has helped to demystify hearing impairments and reduce the stigma often associated with them.

Beyond sharing his personal story, Coleman has been actively involved in various initiatives and organizations that support the deaf community. He has participated in events and campaigns aimed at providing resources and support for individuals with hearing impairments. His involvement in these activities has helped to raise funds, increase awareness, and provide practical support to those in need.

One significant aspect of Coleman's advocacy is his emphasis on the importance of access to education and resources for the deaf and hard-of-hearing. He has highlighted the need for better communication tools, educational opportunities, and support systems that enable individuals with hearing impairments to reach their full potential.

Coleman's impact as an advocate is also noticeable in his capacity as a role model and a source of inspiration. His success in the NFL has shown that hearing impairments do not define a person's capabilities or limit their potential for success. He has become a symbol of resilience and determination, encouraging others to pursue their dreams regardless of the challenges they face.

Moreover, Coleman's advocacy extends to encouraging inclusivity and diversity in sports and beyond. He has been a voice for the importance of creating environments where people with disabilities are included and can thrive. His journey challenges stereotypes and promotes a more inclusive perspective in sports, education, and all areas of society.

Inspiration and Determination

Derrick Coleman's inspiring journey from a young boy with a hearing impairment to a successful NFL player is a powerful narrative that teaches valuable lessons about overcoming personal challenges and achieving dreams. His story exemplifies the virtues of determination, resilience, and the unyielding pursuit of one's goals, regardless of the obstacles.

One of the key lessons from Coleman's story is the importance of self-belief and determination. Facing the challenge of being legally deaf in a sport where communication is crucial, Coleman never let his hearing impairment define him or limit his aspirations. His unwavering belief in his abilities and his determination to succeed in football demonstrate that personal challenges can be overcome with perseverance and a strong sense of self-confidence.

Coleman's journey also highlights the significance of resilience. Throughout his life, he encountered various obstacles, from being undrafted in the NFL to adapting to the demands of professional football with a hearing impairment. His ability to bounce back from setbacks, to adapt and find ways to excel, serves as a lesson in resilience. It shows that challenges, whether physical or situational, can be transformed into stepping stones for success.

Another important aspect of Coleman's story is the power of hard work and preparation. His success in the NFL was not just a result of his talent but also his dedication to honing his skills and preparing himself both physically and mentally for the demands of the game. Coleman's rigorous training and meticulous preparation are examples of how hard work and dedication are critical components in achieving one's dreams.

Moreover, Coleman's story is an inspiration for individuals facing personal challenges of their own. His success serves as a powerful reminder that limitations, whether physical or otherwise, do not have to hinder one's achievements. His journey encourages others to pursue their dreams with determination, regardless of the challenges they may face.

Coleman's influence reaches beyond being a role model. For young people, particularly those with disabilities or facing significant challenges, his story is a source of motivation. It illustrates that with the right mindset, support, and hard work, it is possible to overcome adversity and achieve great things.

The Legend of Jerry Rice

Background and Early Years

Jerry Rice, widely regarded as one of the greatest wide receivers in NFL history, had a humble beginning that belied his future success in professional football. Born on October 13, 1962, in Starkville, Mississippi, Rice grew up in the small town of Crawford. His early life in rural Mississippi was far removed from the glitz and glamour of the NFL, setting the stage for a journey marked by hard work and perseverance.

Rice's introduction to football was somewhat serendipitous. During his high school years at B.L. Moor High School in Oktoc, Mississippi, his speed and athletic ability caught the attention of the school's football coach, who noticed him after Rice was caught being a prankster. His sprinting away from the school's principal demonstrated a natural athleticism that was soon harnessed on the football field.

In high school, Rice quickly developed into a standout player, displaying an early talent for catching the ball and a strong work ethic. Despite his obvious talent, he was not heavily recruited by major college football programs, primarily due to the lack of exposure at his small high school.

Rice's journey to the NFL took a significant turn when he attended Mississippi Valley State University, a small historically black university in Itta Bena. It was here that Rice's talent truly began to shine. Playing for the Delta Devils from 1981 to 1984, he set numerous NCAA records, thanks to his remarkable ability to catch and accumulate yards after the catch. His exceptional performance in college, where he displayed a unique combination of speed, agility, and precise route-running, started to draw attention from NFL scouts.

Despite his stellar college career, questions lingered about the level of competition he faced at a small university, and how well his skills would translate to the professional level. However, Rice's work ethic, combined with his natural talent, would soon quash any doubts, paving his way to an illustrious career in the NFL.

Career Highlights

Rice's professional journey began when he was drafted by the San Francisco 49ers in the first round of the 1985 NFL Draft. Despite a challenging start to his rookie season, he quickly adapted to the NFL's pace and physicality, setting the tone for what would become one of the most storied careers in football history.

One of Rice's most significant achievements is his status as the NFL's all-time leader in receiving yards. Over the course of his career, he amassed an astonishing 22,895 receiving yards, setting a standard for excellence and durability that remains unmatched. This record is a testament to his ability to perform at a high level consistently over a long period.

Rice also holds the record for the most receptions in NFL history. His total of 1,549 receptions reflects his reliability and skill in catching the ball, as well as his longevity in the league. His exceptional hand-eye coordination, precise route running, and ability to make catches in traffic were hallmarks of his playing style.

Another notable record held by Rice is the most touchdown receptions in NFL history, with 197. This remarkable achievement underscores his scoring ability and his knack for finding the end zone. Rice's combination of speed, agility, and understanding of defensive schemes made him a constant scoring threat.

Rice's career was also marked by his performances in high-stakes games. He holds the record for the most receiving yards in Super Bowl history, a testament to his ability to deliver in crucial moments. His Super Bowl performances were often game-changing, including a record-setting three touchdown receptions in Super Bowl XXIV.

In addition to his statistical achievements, what made Rice a phenomenal wide receiver was his meticulous approach to the game. He was renowned for his rigorous offseason training regimen, which included running steep hills to build endurance and strength. This commitment to conditioning contributed significantly to his longevity and productivity on the field.

Rice's ability to excel with different quarterbacks throughout his career also highlighted his adaptability and skill. He maintained his high level of play regardless of changes in the 49ers' and later teams' rosters, demonstrating his universal impact as a receiver.

Work Ethic

Rice's training regimen was famously rigorous and unconventional. He was renowned for his offseason workouts, which were both physically demanding and mentally challenging. One of the most iconic aspects of his training was his hill running. Rice would run a steep hill, known locally as "The Hill," in the San Carlos neighborhood of San Carlos, California. This grueling exercise, which he did throughout his career, was more than just a physical workout; it was a symbol of his determination and commitment to excellence. The hill runs not only built his endurance and strength but also instilled a mental toughness that became a hallmark of his career.

Beyond his physical training, Rice's dedication to perfecting his craft extended to all aspects of his role as a wide receiver. He was meticulous about studying game films, analyzing opponents' defenses, and understanding the nuances of different routes and plays. This deep understanding of the game enabled him to outsmart defenders and consistently find ways to get open.

Rice's practice sessions were known for their intensity. He treated each practice like a game, believing that the habits formed in practice translated directly to performance on the field. His attention to detail in practice, from the precision of his route running to the consistency of his catching, set a standard for the entire team.

His dedication also manifested in his approach to physical conditioning and nutrition. Rice was mindful of his diet and overall fitness, understanding the importance of maintaining peak physical condition to perform at the highest level and extend his career.

Furthermore, Rice's work ethic extended to the offseason, where he famously avoided taking extended breaks, choosing instead to maintain a high level of training. This year-round dedication ensured that he entered each season in top physical and mental shape, ready to perform at his best.

Key Games and Performances

One of Rice's most iconic performances came in Super Bowl XXIII in 1989, where the San Francisco 49ers faced the Cincinnati Bengals. In a game that was fiercely contested, Rice's contribution was monumental. He caught 11 passes for an astonishing 215 yards and scored one touchdown, playing a crucial role in the 49ers' 20-16 victory. His performance earned him the Super Bowl MVP, a rare honor for a wide receiver, and solidified his reputation for delivering in high-stakes situations.

Another notable Super Bowl performance by Rice was in Super Bowl XXIV the following year, against the Denver Broncos. Rice showcased his scoring prowess by catching three touchdown passes, contributing significantly to the 49ers' overwhelming 55-10 victory. This performance further cemented Rice's status as a key player in the 49ers' dynasty and one of the greatest receivers in Super Bowl history.

Rice's impact was not limited to Super Bowls. Throughout his career, he delivered in crucial games. A standout example is the 1994 NFC Championship game against the Dallas Cowboys. In a highly anticipated matchup, Rice made an immediate impact by scoring a 44-yard touchdown on the game's third play. His presence and performance were instrumental in the 49ers' 38-28 win, propelling them to Super Bowl XXIX.

In Super Bowl XXIX against the San Diego Chargers, Rice again proved why he was considered one of the best, catching 10 passes for 149 yards and three touchdowns. His ability to perform under pressure was on full display, helping the 49ers secure a convincing 49-26 victory.

Beyond these marquee games, Rice's career was filled with remarkable performances that showcased his consistency and dominance. He set numerous records, including most touchdowns in a single season and most receiving yards in a single game. Rice's ability to perform at an elite level, game after game, season after season, made him a constant threat on the field and a nightmare for defenses.

Impact on the Game

Rice transformed the wide receiver position through his unparalleled work ethic, route-running precision, and consistent performance. His ability to run routes with exceptional precision made him a master at creating separation from defenders. This aspect of his game, combined with his sure hands and remarkable ability to make catches in traffic, redefined what it meant to be an elite wide receiver. Rice's style of play emphasized the importance of technical skill and intelligence, in addition to physical attributes like speed and strength.

Beyond his on-field skills, Rice's approach to training and preparation had a significant impact on the position. His rigorous offseason workouts, including the notorious hill runs, demonstrated a level of dedication and commitment that was inspirational for other players. Rice showed that being a great wide receiver was not just about natural talent but also about hard work, discipline, and constant self-improvement. His training regimen became a model for wide receivers and other position players who sought to elevate their game.

Rice's influence extended to the strategic aspects of football. His ability to consistently make big plays and impact games forced teams to rethink their defensive strategies. Defenses had to account for Rice in their game plans, often requiring double coverage or specific schemes to try and contain him.

This opened opportunities for other aspects of the offense, showcasing how a dominant wide receiver could change the dynamics of the game.

Furthermore, Rice's success and longevity in the NFL have inspired future generations of wide receivers. He set numerous records, many of which were considered unbreakable, creating a legacy that aspiring players sought to emulate. Rice became a role model for young athletes, not just for his achievements but for the character and professionalism he displayed throughout his career.

His influence can be seen in the way modern wide receivers approach the game. The importance of route running, maintaining peak physical condition, and studying the game are now staples for success at the position, much of which can be attributed to the standard Rice set.

Life Lessons

Jerry Rice's illustrious career and life story impart significant life lessons, particularly emphasizing the importance of hard work, dedication, and the pursuit of excellence. His journey from a modest background to becoming one of the greatest players in NFL history serves as a powerful example of these virtues.

The lesson of hard work is central to Rice's story. His relentless work ethic, both during the season and in the off-season, was a critical factor in his success. Rice's commitment to training, whether it was running challenging hill workouts or spending extra hours catching balls after practice, demonstrated that success in any field requires consistent and focused effort. His approach underscores the idea that while talent is valuable, it is hard work that often makes the difference between good and great.

Dedication is another key lesson from Rice's career. Throughout his years in the NFL, Rice remained committed to his goals, never settling for anything less than his best. He was dedicated not only to improving his physical skills but also to understanding the game's strategic aspects. This dedication extended to his diet, physical conditioning, and mental preparation, showing that true excellence requires a holistic and unwavering commitment to one's craft.

Rice's career also teaches the importance of the pursuit of excellence. He constantly set high standards for himself, striving to be the best player he could be. This pursuit was not about complacency or resting on his laurels; even after achieving significant milestones, Rice continued to push himself. His career exemplifies the idea that the pursuit of excellence is a continuous journey, not a destination.

Additionally, Rice's journey teaches resilience and the ability to overcome challenges. Facing initial difficulties in his rookie season, he demonstrated the ability to learn from mistakes and bounce back stronger. This resilience is a pivotal life lesson, emphasizing that setbacks can be opportunities for growth and improvement.

Moreover, Rice's story is an inspiration for setting and achieving goals. He had a clear vision of what he wanted to accomplish and diligently worked towards those goals. His success shows that with a clear focus and the willingness to put in the necessary effort, achieving one's dreams is possible.

The Iron Will of Brett Favre

Rise to Fame

Brett Favre's rise to fame in the NFL is a compelling story of resilience, talent, and an iron will, which saw him transform from a second-round draft pick into one of the most iconic quarterbacks in football history. His journey is marked by a combination of raw skill, sheer determination, and a charismatic playing style that captivated fans and players alike.

Favre's journey began in Gulfport, Mississippi, where he was born on October 10, 1969. He later played college football at the University of Southern Mississippi. Despite initially being overlooked by bigger college programs, Favre made his mark at Southern Mississippi. His time in college was characterized by his gritty play and ability to produce remarkable comebacks, traits that would become hallmarks of his NFL career. His fearless playing style and strong arm caught the attention of NFL scouts, despite concerns about his rawness and decision-making.

Favre was selected by the Atlanta Falcons in the second round of the 1991 NFL Draft. However, his time with the Falcons was brief and uneventful, as he struggled to find playing time. The turning point in Favre's career came when he was traded to the Green Bay Packers in 1992. This move would prove to be pivotal, not just for Favre, but for the Packers franchise as a whole.

Once with the Packers, Favre's career trajectory changed dramatically. Thrust into the starting role early in his tenure, Favre quickly began to showcase his exceptional abilities. His arm strength, durability, and instinctive style of play made him stand out. Favre's willingness to take risks, sometimes resulting in spectacular plays and other times in costly interceptions, became a defining aspect of his game.

Favre's rise to fame was marked by a series of remarkable seasons with the Packers. He led the team to multiple playoff appearances and was instrumental in revitalizing a storied franchise that had experienced years of mediocrity. Favre's fearless approach, combined with his leadership and ability to perform in clutch situations, endeared him to fans and earned him respect across the league.

One of the most significant milestones in Favre's career was leading the Packers to victory in Super Bowl XXXI. This achievement not only cemented his status as an elite quarterback but also marked the resurgence of the Packers as a powerhouse in the NFL.

Resilience and Grit

Brett Favre's resilience and grit are epitomized by his record for consecutive starts, a remarkable feat that underscores his toughness and commitment to the game. Favre's streak of starting in 297 regular season games (321 including playoffs), spanning from 1992 to 2010, stands as a testament to his physical and mental durability.

Favre's streak of consecutive starts is not just a number; it's a narrative of playing through numerous injuries and personal tragedies, reflecting his extraordinary resilience. Over the years, he sustained various injuries that would have sidelined most players, including thumb sprains, ankle sprains, a separated shoulder, and even a broken thumb. Despite these ailments, Favre remained undeterred, often delivering some of his best performances under physical duress.

His ability to play through pain was not just about physical toughness; it also spoke to his mental grit. Favre's commitment to his team and the game was unwavering, as he consistently put the team's success ahead of his physical discomfort. This relentless drive was a source of inspiration for his teammates and a demonstration of his leadership.

Moreover, Favre's resilience was also evident in how he dealt with personal tragedies while maintaining his high level of play. One of the most poignant examples was his performance in a game against the Oakland Raiders in 2003, a day after his father, Irvin Favre, passed away. In an emotionally charged game, Favre threw for 399 yards and four touchdowns in a performance that is remembered as one of the most courageous and poignant in NFL history.

Favre's ability to maintain his consecutive starts streak also required a rigorous and disciplined approach to physical conditioning and recovery. He was proactive in his approach to injury treatment and rehabilitation, ensuring that he remained in the best possible shape to continue his streak.

Signature Playing Style

Brett Favre's signature playing style, characterized by an aggressive, risk-taking approach, made him one of the most exciting and dynamic quarterbacks in NFL history. His style of play was marked by a unique combination of raw arm strength, improvisational ability, and a willingness to take chances that few quarterbacks would dare.

Favre's arm strength was legendary. He could make throws that few others could, firing the ball downfield with remarkable velocity and accuracy. This ability allowed him to attempt and complete passes in situations where other quarterbacks might not have even tried. Favre's fearless approach to throwing deep and into tight coverage became a defining feature of his game, thrilling fans and often catching defenses off guard.

His risk-taking style was both a strength and a vulnerability. Favre was known for attempting difficult throws, leading to spectacular plays but also resulting in a high number of interceptions. This gunslinger mentality – the willingness to take chances in pursuit of big plays – made every game unpredictable and exhilarating. While his aggressive style sometimes led to mistakes, it also resulted in some of the most memorable moments in football.

One such moment was the 1996 NFC Championship Game against the Carolina Panthers, where Favre's aggressive play was on full display. He threw for two touchdowns and 292 yards, leading the Packers to a victory and securing their place in Super Bowl XXXI. His performance in that game encapsulated his ability to make game-changing plays.

Another memorable moment was in a Monday Night Football game against the Oakland Raiders in 2003. Playing just one day after his father's death, Favre threw for 399 yards and four touchdowns in an emotionally charged performance that is widely regarded as one of the greatest in NFL history. This game showcased not just his physical skills but also his emotional resilience and leadership.

Favre's improvisational skills were also a key aspect of his playing style. He had a knack for making plays out of broken situations, often turning potential sacks or losses into big gains. His ability to extend plays with his feet and make off-balance throws added an unpredictable element to his game that was both thrilling and effective.

Challenges and Controversies

One of the major challenges Favre faced on the field was his propensity for interceptions. His aggressive, risk-taking playing style, while often leading to spectacular plays, also resulted in a high number of turnovers. Favre holds the NFL record for most career interceptions, a testament to both his longevity and his high-risk approach to the game. This aspect of his play was often a point of criticism and a challenge he had to continually address throughout his career.

Off the field, Favre faced several controversies. One of the most significant was in 2010, involving allegations of sending inappropriate messages and photos to a Jets game-day hostess while he was with the New York Jets. The scandal garnered widespread media attention and led to an NFL investigation, which resulted in Favre being fined for failing to cooperate with the investigation. This incident marred Favre's reputation and became a talking point in discussions about his legacy.

Another challenge for Favre was his series of retirements and comebacks. Towards the end of his career, he announced his retirement multiple times, only to return to play again. These indecisions, particularly around his time with the Packers and later with the Jets and Minnesota Vikings, led to media scrutiny and some criticism from fans and analysts. His wavering on retirement decisions created uncertainty and controversy both for him and the teams involved.

Favre also dealt with personal challenges, including struggles with addiction. Early in his career, he developed an addiction to painkillers, which he publicly acknowledged and sought treatment for in the mid-1990s. This battle with addiction showed a vulnerable side to Favre and highlighted the pressures and challenges faced by professional athletes.

Additionally, Favre's long career in the NFL was not without its physical toll. He endured numerous injuries, some of which were severe. His ability to play through pain and maintain his consecutive starts streak was as much a testament to his toughness as it was a source of concern for his long-term health.

Retirement and Legacy

Brett Favre's retirement and unretirement saga, along with his overall legacy in the NFL, paint a picture of a legendary player whose career was marked by both remarkable achievements and unique challenges. Favre's journey through the final years of his career and his ultimate retirement left an indelible mark on the NFL landscape.

Favre first announced his retirement from the NFL in March 2008, after 16 seasons with the Green Bay Packers. This announcement was met with a wave of tributes, reflecting his status as one of the greatest quarterbacks in the history of the league. However, this retirement was short-lived, as Favre returned to the NFL just a few months later, creating a significant stir in the sports world. He joined the New York Jets for the 2008 season, adding another chapter to his storied career.

After a single season with the Jets, Favre again announced his retirement, only to make another comeback with the Minnesota Vikings in 2009. His tenure with the Vikings was marked by some high-level performances, including leading the team to the NFC Championship Game. Favre's ability to perform at an elite level, even after multiple retirements, was a testament to his enduring skill and passion for the game.

Favre's final retirement came in 2010, after a 20-year career in the NFL. This marked the end of a journey that was as tumultuous as it was illustrious. Despite the controversies and challenges, Favre's retirement was met with widespread recognition of his contributions to the sport.

Favre's overall legacy in the NFL is significant. He left the game as one of its most prolific passers, holding numerous records at the time of his retirement, including the most career passing yards, most career touchdown passes, and most career pass completions. His record for consecutive starts, 297 regular season games (321 including playoffs), is a remarkable feat that exemplifies his durability and toughness.

Beyond the statistics, Favre's legacy is also defined by his playing style and persona. His gunslinger mentality, willingness to take risks, and ability to make extraordinary plays under pressure made him a fan favorite and a respected figure among his peers. Favre's passion for the game, evident in his energetic and enthusiastic playing style, endeared him to fans and brought a unique excitement to the sport.

Inspiring Perseverance

Brett Favre's career provides a powerful narrative on inspiring perseverance, offering valuable lessons on determination, facing adversity, and achieving longevity in one's endeavors. His journey in the NFL is a testament to the relentless pursuit of goals in the face of challenges, both personal and professional.

A key lesson from Favre's career is the importance of unwavering determination. Throughout his time in the NFL, Favre exhibited an extraordinary commitment to the sport he loved. This was evident in his willingness to play through injuries, personal struggles, and the constant pressure of professional sports. Favre's determination to succeed, regardless of the obstacles, highlights the importance of resilience and a strong will in achieving success.

Favre's career also teaches valuable lessons about facing adversity. His ability to bounce back from setbacks, whether they were poor performances, injuries, or personal struggles, demonstrates how challenges can be transformed into opportunities for growth. Favre's approach to adversity was not one of avoidance, but of confronting it head-on, learning from it, and emerging stronger. This mindset is crucial not just in sports, but in all areas of life where challenges are inevitable.

Another aspect of Favre's career that stands out is his longevity in a highly competitive and physically demanding sport. Achieving a two-decade-long career in the NFL, marked by consistent high-level performance, is a remarkable feat. This longevity can be attributed to Favre's meticulous approach to physical conditioning, mental preparation, and his ability to adapt his playing style over the years. Favre's career longevity serves as a reminder of the importance of taking care of oneself, continuously learning, and adapting to maintain relevance and effectiveness in any field.

Furthermore, Favre's journey underscores the importance of passion and love for what one does. His enthusiasm for football was infectious and a driving force behind his long career. This passion was a source of motivation that kept him going through the ups and downs of his career. It teaches that finding and nurturing a passion can be a powerful motivator and a key to long-term success.

The Revolutionary Tony Dungy

Early Career and Challenges

Born on October 6, 1955, in Jackson, Michigan, Dungy grew up in a family where education and character were emphasized. His early life was marked by a strong work ethic and a passion for football. Dungy played quarterback at Parkside High School in Jackson, showcasing early signs of the leadership and strategic thinking that would define his career. He then went on to play college football at the University of Minnesota, where he continued to play as a quarterback.

Despite a successful college career, Dungy faced challenges upon entering the NFL. In 1977, he joined the Pittsburgh Steelers as a free agent but was moved from quarterback to defensive back due to the prevailing biases and stereotypes about the quarterback position. Dungy's adaptability was on display as he made the transition to defense, demonstrating his versatility and football intelligence.

Dungy's playing career in the NFL included stints with the Steelers and the San Francisco 49ers. While he was not a standout player in the league, his understanding of the game and leadership qualities were evident. It was these attributes that laid the foundation for his transition to coaching.

After his playing career, Dungy embarked on a coaching journey that began in 1981, serving in various assistant coaching roles with the Steelers, Kansas City Chiefs, and Minnesota Vikings. His rise through the coaching ranks was marked by his calm demeanor, sharp defensive acumen, and ability to inspire and motivate players. Dungy quickly gained respect in coaching circles for his strategic mind and his unique approach to leadership.

Dungy's early coaching career was also a time when he faced and overcame significant challenges. As an African American coach in a league where diversity in leadership positions was limited, Dungy broke barriers and paved the way for future generations of coaches. His perseverance in the face of these challenges was not just a personal victory but a step forward in the fight for greater diversity and inclusion in the NFL.

Coaching Philosophy

Dungy's calm demeanor on the sidelines was one of his most notable traits. Unlike many of his contemporaries, he rarely displayed anger or frustration publicly. This composure under pressure created a stable and focused environment for his players, fostering a sense of confidence and clarity during games. Dungy believed that maintaining a calm presence helped his players perform at their best, as it allowed them to concentrate on the game without the added pressure of an emotionally reactive coach.

Central to Dungy's philosophy was the emphasis on character. He firmly believed that the key to success on the field was building a team of individuals who were not only talented athletes but also possessed strong moral character. Dungy often spoke about the importance of discipline, responsibility, and teamwork, and he sought players who embodied these values. He was known for his ability to inspire his players to strive for excellence both on and off the field.

Dungy's leadership style was also characterized by his emphasis on leading by example. He treated players, staff, and opponents with respect and expected the same from those around him. This approach earned him immense respect from his players and peers, as they saw him as a coach who practiced what he preached. His integrity and consistency in this regard were instrumental in building trust and loyalty among his team members.

Moreover, Dungy's coaching philosophy extended beyond the X's and O's of football. He was a mentor to many of his players, offering guidance and support in their personal lives as well. Dungy's holistic approach to coaching was about developing his players not just as athletes but as individuals. He believed that personal growth was crucial to team success.

His philosophy also included a focus on teamwork and collective success over individual achievements. Dungy emphasized the importance of each team member's role and the power of working together towards a common goal. This team-first mentality was a cornerstone of his coaching approach and was evident in the way his teams played.

Breaking Racial Barriers

Dungy's success in leading the Colts to a Super Bowl victory was a groundbreaking moment in the history of the league. For decades, African American coaches had faced significant challenges and obstacles in the NFL, often struggling to secure head coaching positions due to systemic biases and a lack of opportunities. Dungy's victory shattered a longstanding racial barrier, demonstrating unequivocally that African American coaches could achieve the highest levels of success in the sport.

The significance of Dungy's accomplishment extends to its impact on diversity and inclusion within the NFL. His victory served as a powerful symbol of progress and a beacon of hope for aspiring coaches of color. It challenged the status quo and sparked conversations about the importance of diversity in coaching and leadership positions in sports. Dungy's success helped pave the way for other African American coaches, inspiring them to pursue their coaching aspirations and proving that race should not be a barrier to achieving coaching excellence.

Moreover, Dungy's achievement in Super Bowl XLI was a source of pride and inspiration for the African American community. It represented a moment of triumph over historical racial barriers and prejudices, offering a vivid example of perseverance and excellence. Dungy's victory was not just celebrated as a sporting achievement but also as a significant step forward in the broader struggle for racial equality and representation.

Importantly, Dungy's approach to breaking racial barriers was characterized by his grace and integrity. He led by example, focusing on his coaching abilities and leadership qualities rather than allowing his race to define his career. His professionalism and dedication to the sport were key factors in his success, earning him respect from players, peers, and fans alike.

Mentorship and Impact

Dungy's mentorship style was characterized by his focus on character development and personal growth. He believed that a coach's role extended beyond teaching the technical aspects of the game; it also involved nurturing players and coaches as individuals. This approach led him to invest deeply in the personal and professional development of those he mentored, providing guidance, support, and wisdom.

For players, Dungy was more than a coach; he was a role model and a father figure. He took a keen interest in their lives outside of football, offering advice and support in areas ranging from financial management to personal relationships. His focus on building strong character was evident in the way he encouraged players to be responsible, disciplined, and community-oriented. Many players credited Dungy with not only helping them improve their game but also with making them better people.

Dungy also played a pivotal role in mentoring other coaches, particularly African American coaches. He was instrumental in promoting diversity within the coaching ranks, using his influence to open doors and provide opportunities for minority coaches. Dungy's mentorship helped prepare the next generation of coaches, equipping them with the skills, knowledge, and values necessary to succeed in the NFL.

One of Dungy's most notable mentees is Mike Tomlin, whom Dungy hired as a defensive backs coach with the Tampa Bay Buccaneers. Tomlin, who would go on to become the head coach of the Pittsburgh Steelers and win a Super Bowl, often spoke of the profound impact Dungy had on his career and life. Dungy's mentorship of Tomlin is just one example of his broader impact on the coaching community.

Dungy's influence extended beyond the individuals he directly mentored. His leadership style and philosophy had a ripple effect throughout the NFL, inspiring other coaches and players to adopt similar approaches. His emphasis on integrity, humility, and the importance of balancing professional success with personal well-being has left a lasting mark on the sport.

Personal Life and Advocacy

Tony Dungy's personal life, marked by strong family values and advocacy for various causes, reflects the depth of his character and his commitment to making a positive impact beyond the football field. His personal endeavors provide insight into the man behind the coaching legend, revealing a life dedicated to family, faith, and community service.

Family has always been a central aspect of Dungy's life. He and his wife, Lauren, have been deeply involved in their children's lives, emphasizing the importance of family bonds and shared values. Dungy's approach to fatherhood mirrors his approach to coaching, focusing on character development, guidance, and leading by example. He has often spoken about the importance of balancing his professional responsibilities with his role as a husband and father, striving to be present and involved in his family's life.

Dungy's faith is another cornerstone of his personal life. A devout Christian, his faith has shaped his worldview and his approach to both his professional career and personal endeavors. He has been open about the role of faith in guiding his decisions and actions, emphasizing themes of forgiveness, compassion, and service to others. Dungy's faith has been a source of strength and inspiration throughout his life, influencing his interactions and choices.

In addition to his family and faith, Dungy has been a vocal advocate for various causes. He has used his platform to promote and support community service, education, and youth development programs. Dungy has been involved in numerous charitable activities, including work with organizations focused on children and families, mentoring initiatives, and programs aimed at improving the lives of disadvantaged youth.

One of Dungy's significant advocacy roles has been his involvement in prison ministries and efforts to support formerly incarcerated individuals. He has been passionate about helping these individuals reintegrate into society and rebuild their lives, reflecting his belief in redemption and second chances.

Dungy has also been an advocate for mental health awareness, particularly in the wake of personal tragedy. After the loss of his son, James, to suicide, Dungy and his family have been open about their experiences with grief and mental health. They have worked to break down the stigma surrounding mental health issues and have encouraged open discussions about seeking help and support.

Furthermore, Dungy has been an influential voice in discussions about race, diversity, and inclusion, both within the NFL and in broader society. His experiences as an African American coach and his commitment to promoting diversity and equality have made him a respected figure in conversations about these critical issues.

Legacy Beyond the Field

Tony Dungy's legacy extends far beyond the football field, characterized by his unwavering integrity, exceptional leadership, and deep commitment to community involvement. His influence in these areas has made a lasting impact, shaping not just the world of sports but also the broader societal landscape.

Dungy's integrity has been a defining feature of his legacy. In a profession often marked by intense pressure and high stakes, Dungy consistently maintained his principles, both in his coaching career and personal life. He is widely respected for his ethical approach to coaching, prioritizing character and moral values over winning at any cost. This commitment to integrity has set a standard in the NFL and has been a guiding light for coaches, players, and fans alike.

In terms of leadership, Dungy's influence has been profound. His leadership style, characterized by calmness, respect, and positivity, has redefined what it means to be a successful leader in the high-pressure environment of professional sports. Dungy's approach to leadership, focusing on mentorship, personal development, and leading by example, has been emulated by many in and out of sports. His emphasis on the importance of being a role model has inspired countless individuals to adopt a similar approach in their leadership roles.

Dungy's community involvement has also been a significant aspect of his legacy. He has been actively involved in various charitable and community initiatives, using his platform to advocate for important causes and to make a positive difference in the lives of others. His work with children and families, educational programs, and support for formerly incarcerated individuals has had a tangible impact on communities. Dungy's commitment to community service exemplifies how individuals can use their influence to effect positive change.

Additionally, Dungy's role in promoting mental health awareness and his advocacy for diversity and inclusion have extended his impact beyond the football arena. By speaking openly about personal challenges and championing the cause of equality, Dungy has contributed to important societal conversations and initiatives. His efforts in these areas have helped to break down stigmas and promote a more inclusive and understanding society.

Dungy's legacy is also evident in the way he has inspired others to pursue their goals with integrity, humility, and a commitment to excellence. His life story and career serve as powerful examples of how perseverance, grounded in strong values, can lead to success and fulfillment.

References

Young, Jeff C. *Devin Hester*. Mason Crest Publishers (2009)

Mendiola, Jordan. *The Complete Story of Tom Brady (The GOAT)*. Medium (2022). https://medium.com/long-term-perspective/the-complete-story-of-tom-brady-36cb0c89be41. Accessed December 02, 2023

Moyer, Susan M. *Reggie White: A Celebration of Life, 1961-2004*. Sports Publishing LLC (2005)

Mullen, Robert. *The Greatest Show on Turf: The Story of 99-01 St. Louis Rams*. Outskirts Press, Incorporated (2009)

Heits, Rudolph T. *Jason Witten*. Mason Crest Publishers (2010)

Parker, John. *Vince Lombardi: Everything That Is Great About Football*. Bleacher Report (2008). https://bleacherreport.com/articles/82038-vince-lombardi-everything-that-is-great-about-football. Accessed November 29, 2023

Borelli, Stephen. *The story of Doug Williams, celebrated now, was hardly a fairy tale: He faced ugly racism*. USA TODAY (2023). https://www.usatoday.com/story/sports/nfl/super-bowl/2023/02/12/doug-williams-story-celebrated-now-hardly-fairy-tale/11238198002/. Accessed November 30, 2023

Turner, Mark Tye. *Notes from a 12 Man: A Truly Biased History of the Seattle Seahawks*. Sasquatch Books (2010)

Fantasy Boss. *New England Patriots 2016 Super Bowl LI Champion Season Statistic Logbook: All Game And Individual Statistics From The 2016 Season*. CreateSpace Independent Publishing Platform (2017)

Taylor, Roy. *Walter Payton, Bears RB, 1975-1987*. Bears History (2002). http://www.bearshistory.com/lore/walterpayton.aspx. Accessed Dec 03, 2023

Willard, Samuel. *Peyton Manning*. Chelsea House (2015).

Dulac, Gerry. *Catch of a lifetime: Legendary 'Immaculate Reception' lives on 50 years later*. Pro Football Hall of Fame (2023). https://www.profootballhof.com/news/2022/catch-of-a-lifetime-legendary-immaculate-reception-lives-on-50-years-later/. Accessed December 04, 2023

Bishop, Chad. *A First for Fuller ... and for All*. Vu Commodores (2020). https://vucommodores.com/a-first-for-fuller-and-for-all/. Accessed November 28, 2023

Gruver, Ed. *The Ice Bowl: The Cold Truth About Football's Most Unforgettable Game*. Lyons Press (2021)

Bordow, Scott. *Cardinals fullback Derrick Coleman is deaf and was bullied as a kid; now he has a Super Bowl ring*. The Athletic (2018). https://theathletic.com/680028/2018/11/28/cardinals-fullback-derrick-coleman-is-deaf-and-was-bullied-as-a-kid-now-he-has-a-super-bowl-ring/. Accessed November 30, 2023

Beard, Alison. *Life's Work: An Interview with Jerry Rice*. Harvard Business Review (2022). https://hbr.org/2022/09/lifes-work-an-interview-with-jerry-rice. Accessed December 05, 2023

Koestler-Grack, Rachel A. *Brett Favre*. Chelsea House Publisher (2015).

Fischer, Ben. *Tony Dungy: The Conscience of the NFL*. Sports Business Journal (2021). https://www.sportsbusinessjournal.com/Journal/Issues/2021/09/20/Champions/Dungy.aspx. Accessed December 01, 2023

Bonus: Free Book!

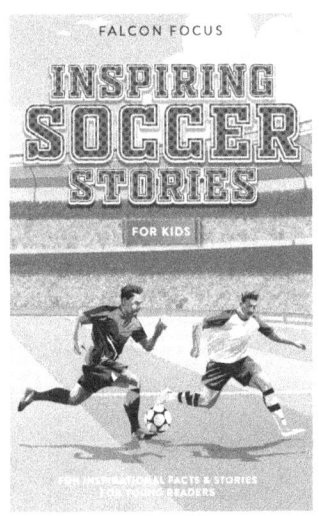

Are you ready to delve into the *Inspiring Soccer Stories* for free? Get ready to go deep into the world soccer? Just use your smartphone or tablet to scan the QR code below, then follow the simple prompts to receive the PDF.

www.ingramcontent.com/pod-product-compliance
Lightning Source LLC
Chambersburg PA
CBHW052059110526
44591CB00013B/2271